History SL&HL
FOR THE IB DIPLOMA

The Move to Global War

Joe Gauci

PEAK

Published by:
Peak Study Resources Ltd
1 & 3 Kings Meadow
Oxford OX2 0DP
UK

www.peakib.com

History SL & HL The Move to Global War: Study & Revision Guide for the IB Diploma

ISBN 978-1-913433-37-6

© Joe Gauci 2017–21

Joe Gauci has asserted his right under the Copyright, Design and Patents Act 1988 to be identified as the author of this work.

All rights reserved. No part of this publication may be reproduced, stored in a retrieval system, or transmitted in any form or by any means, without the prior permission of the publishers.

PHOTOCOPYING ANY PAGES FROM THIS PUBLICATION,
EXCEPT UNDER LICENCE, IS PROHIBITED

Peak Study & Revision Guides for the IB Diploma have been developed independently of the International Baccalaureate Organization (IBO). 'International Baccalaureate' and 'IB' are registered trademarks of the IBO.

Books may be ordered directly from the publisher (see www.peakib.com) and through online or local booksellers. For enquiries regarding titles, availability or retailers, please email books@peakib.com or use the form at www.peakib.com/contact.

Printed and bound in the UK by:
CPI Group (UK) Ltd, Croydon CR0 4YY
www.cpibooks.co.uk

Cover image: Political Instability (kentoh via Adobe Stock)

This study and revision guide is the fifth that I have produced for History Paper 1 over the past ten years. I have particularly enjoyed writing these, as source analysis is something I have always found hugely engaging. My fascination with working with sources dates back to my days as a student at Oxford University in the early 1980s, where I had the opportunity to get a sense of what being a 'real' historian was like, by being able to delve in to collections of primary sources in the Bodleian Library, particularly relating to the English Civil War and my great historical hero, Oliver Cromwell.

Since then, source evaluation has invariably been the area of my teaching that I have most looked forward to. I have taught History for the past thirty years in independent schools in the UK, including teaching the IB for twenty-three years at Malvern College, as well as teaching on Oxford Study Courses' Easter and Summer revision courses for the past twenty years. I am never happier than when discussing sources with students, exchanging ideas about the insights they can provide into the past and trying to get them to think critically about what the sources can and can't tell us about the past. So, working on this study guide has been a real pleasure, and I have tried to take approaches in writing it that my experience over the past thirty years has shown to work best in preparing students to tackle source-based questions.

I hope you find the guide a real help in preparing for your Paper 1 examination and also hope that you will find it interesting and informative.

Good luck!

Joe Gauci

Acknowledgements

I would like to thank Peter Jackson for his kindness in reviewing this guide and offering suggestions for improvements. Any errors, I hasten to add, are entirely my own.

I would also like to thank Solo Syndication, London, for their kind permission to use David Low's cartoon 'Trial by Geneva', 24 November 1932, Evening Standard.

Dedication

To all of my colleagues at Oxford Study Courses I offer my thanks for all of their support and friendship over the past 20 years. I dedicate this revision guide to them. I have had a wonderful time working on OSC's spring and summer revision courses.

Contents

How to use this guide v

Advice on Tackling Paper 1 vii

Chapter 1: Case Study: Japanese Expansion in East Asia (1931–1941) 1

    1.1 Causes of Expansion   1

        1.1.1 The Impact of Japanese Nationalism and Militarism on Foreign Policy   1

        1.1.2 Japanese Domestic Issues: Political and Economic Issues, and Their Impact on Foreign Relations   10

        1.1.3 Political Instability in China   12

    1.2 EVENTS: The Japanese Invasion of Manchuria and Northern China (1931)   13

        1.2.1 RESPONSES: The League of Nations and the Lytton Report   14

    1.3 EVENTS: Sino-Japanese War (1937–1941)   16

        1.3.1 RESPONSES: Political Developments within China—the Second United Front   22

    1.4 EVENTS: The Three Power/Tripartite Pact (1940); the Outbreak of War; Pearl Harbor (1941)   25

        1.4.1 RESPONSES: International Response, including US Initiatives and Increasing Tensions between the US and Japan   29

    1.5 Suggested Points for Practice Questions on Japanese Expansion   31

    1.6 A Complete Set of Practice Source-based Questions: The Manchurian Crisis   32

        1.6.1 Questions   33

        1.6.2 Some Suggested Responses   34

Chapter 2: Case Study: German and Italian Expansion (1933–1940) 37

    2.1 Causes of Expansion   37

        2.1.1 The Impact of Fascism on Italy's Foreign Policy   37

        2.1.2 The Impact of Nazism on Germany's Foreign Policy   40

        2.1.3 The Impact of Domestic Economic Issues on the Foreign Policies of Italy and Germany   42

        2.1.4 Changing Diplomatic Alignments in Europe   43

        2.1.5 The End of Collective Security   44

        2.1.6 Appeasement   46

    2.2 EVENTS: German Challenges to the Post-war Settlements (1933–1938)   48

        2.2.1 RESPONSES: International Response to German Aggression (1933–1938)   54

    2.3 EVENTS: German Expansion (1938–1939); Nazi-Soviet Pact, and the Outbreak of War   63

        2.3.1 RESPONSES: International Response to German Aggression (1939–1940)   66

    2.4 EVENTS: Italian Expansion: Abyssinia (1935–1936)   74

        2.4.1 RESPONSES: International Response to Italian Aggression (1935–1936)   76

    2.5 EVENTS: Italian Intervention in the Spanish Civil War (1936)   78

    2.6 EVENTS: Mussolini Establishes Closer Relations with Nazi Germany   79

2.7	EVENTS: The Sudeten Crisis and the Munich Conference (1938)	80
2.8	EVENTS: The Invasion of Albania (7 April 1939)	81
	2.8.1 RESPONSES: France and Britain's Response to Italy's Invasion of Albania	81
2.9	EVENTS: The Pact of Steel (May 1939)	81
2.10	EVENTS: Italy's Entry into World War Two (10 June 1940)	83
2.11	EVENTS and RESPONSES: Italian Aggression in 1940–1941; Britain's and Germany's Responses	84
2.12	Suggested Points for Exam Practice Questions on Italian and German Expansion	85
2.13	A Complete Set of Practice Source-based Questions: The Abyssinian Crisis	87
	2.13.1 Questions	88
	2.13.2 Mark Scheme	89

Appendix **93**

How to use this guide

Success on IB History Paper 1 requires a combination of mastery of a range of techniques in answering the source-based questions and a secure understanding of the two case studies that make up the prescribed subject. In terms of technique, the guide starts with a section of advice on how to approach each of the four types of Paper 1 question, helping you to understand the demands of each question, and what the examiners will be looking for. In addition, throughout this guide I have provided a number of Paper 1-style questions for you to practise on and also, at the end of each case study, suggested points that could be made to secure full marks in answering those questions.

I would recommend that you:

- first try answering the practice questions
- and then look at my suggestions and compare them with what you have come up with.

At the end of each case study, there is a full set of source-based questions for you to practise on. Again, I would recommend that you:

- start by either producing some bullet-point answers or answers in full
- and then look at my suggested answers and comments which follow on from the practice questions.

In order to understand confidently the sources that you will be tackling in the examination paper, you will need a secure knowledge and understanding of the factual content of the two case studies. A detailed knowledge of the key events and developments is also explicitly required for Question 4, which demands that you use your own knowledge as well as the sources. This guide aims to provide you with a very clear explanation of the course content for Paper 1, and I have structured the guide's sections around the bullet points in the syllabus, meaning that there is a good set of notes on every bullet point around which the IBO will set the examination paper. Providing you with only a brief outline of events simply would not equip you to access the top marks on Paper 1, so I have quite deliberately incorporated sufficient information that would enable you to answer questions in depth on any part of the syllabus. However, I have balanced that depth by focusing exclusively on the syllabus bullet points, and nothing else, as well as by providing you with plenty of practice question opportunities and technical tips for answering Paper 1-style questions. Where some words or key terms may not be familiar to you, I have incorporated definition boxes on the relevant pages.

Navigating the guide

This guide is structured to enable you to study efficiently:

- **key terms** are highlighted in bold,
- additional information such as **timelines** and **key questions** appear as a discrete section in the text with colour-coded start and end markers,
- **practice questions** follow the relevant sections of text.

We use icons to help you quickly and easily identify different types of information.

Key to icons used in this study guide

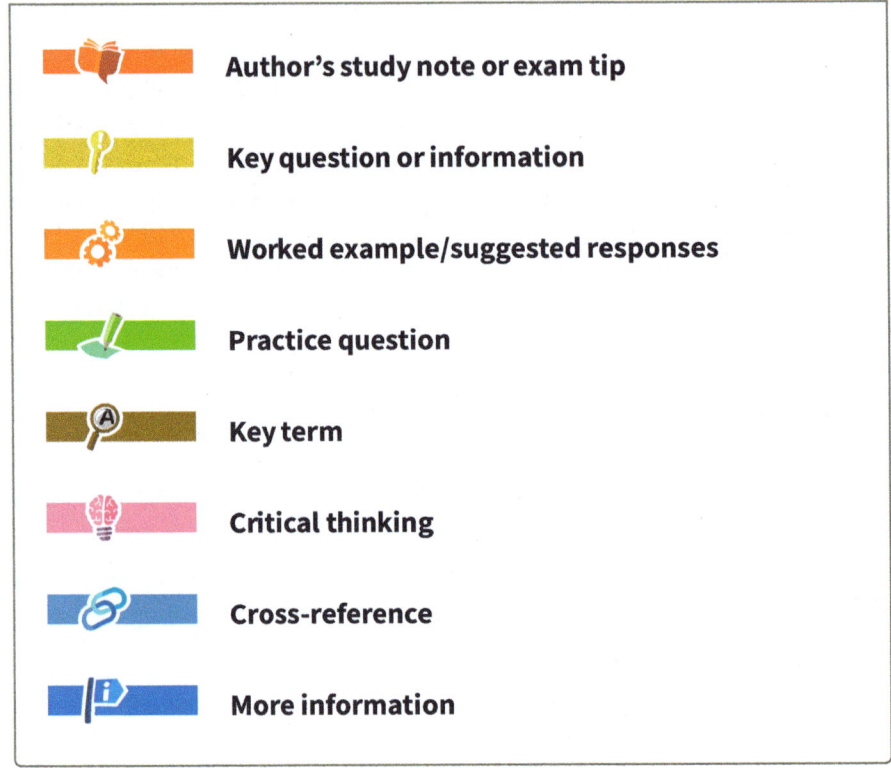

Advice on Tackling Paper 1

What is Paper 1?

Paper 1 is a source-based paper set on prescribed subjects.

Each prescribed subject consists of two specified case studies; for each examination session, the examination paper will focus on one of the two case studies.

The paper will contain *four* sources.

You must answer all four questions; they are worth a total of 24 marks.

The examination lasts 1 hour and makes up 20% of the assessment for Higher Level and 30% of the assessment for Standard Level.

Is there any information on particular topic areas within each prescribed subject that the International Baccalaureate Organization (IBO) will set the source questions on?

Yes. The IBO have included in the History Syllabus a list of topic areas on which the source questions will be based. I have listed the topic areas at the end of this Advice section.

What types of source will be included on the examination paper?

They will be either primary (sources produced at the time of an event) or a mixture of primary and secondary (sources produced after the event by someone who was not there at the time the event occurred).

They may consist of written sources (e.g. letters, the text of a speech, extracts from books), visual sources (e.g. paintings, cartoons, photos), diagrams and statistical information.

What type of questions will be set?

Question 1 is in two parts (a) and (b).
- Both parts (a) and (b) test your understanding of one of the sources.
- Question 1 is worth **5 marks**: part (a) is worth 3 marks and part (b) is worth 2.
- Part (a) will be phrased along the lines of: 'According to Source A (or B or C or D), why...?'
- Part (b) will ask 'What message is conveyed by Source...?'

HISTORY SL & HL: THE MOVE TO GLOBAL WAR

Question 2

- It will ask you to assess the value and limitations of one source with reference to the source's origins, purpose and content, e.g. 'With reference to its origins, purpose and content, assess the value and limitations of Source B to an historian studying Mussolini's invasion of Abyssinia.'
- It is worth **4 marks**.

Question 3

- It will ask you to compare and contrast what two of the sources reveal about a particular aspect of the case study, e.g. 'Compare and contrast what Sources A and Source C reveal about the reasons why Britain followed a policy of appeasement.'
- It is worth **6 marks**.

Question 4

- It will ask you to use your own knowledge and the sources to construct an argument in answer to a question about the prescribed subject, e.g. 'Using the sources and your own knowledge, evaluate the consequences of Japan's invasion of Manchuria.'
- It is worth **9 marks**.

Advice on answering questions

- Write in complete sentences.
- Use the mark allocation for each question to determine how long you spend on each question. In particular, give yourself enough time to do justice to Question 4 as it is worth 9 marks out of the total of 24.

  A rough guide, might be to spend:
    - about 11 minutes on Question 1 (worth 5 marks)
    - about 10 minutes on Question 2 (worth 4 marks)
    - about 15 minutes on Question 3 (worth 6 marks)
    - about 22–24 minutes on Question 4 (worth 9 marks).

- Remember to judge each individual source on its merits or weaknesses; avoid generalisations like 'Source A is a secondary source and so is unreliable because the author will not know exactly what happened.' Both primary and secondary sources can be reliable or unreliable. Also, just because a source is biased does not mean it is of no use to an historian. For example, a speech by Hitler about the Non-Aggression Pact with the USSR might not provide the historian with objective information about the pact, but it might tell us something very useful about the way in which Hitler wanted to project the pact to the world.

Question 1

- In answering this **comprehension** type of question, you need to remember to use just the source, not your own knowledge. In this type of question, the examiners are testing your understanding of the source. It is better if you keep direct quotations from the passage brief and avoid quoting back whole chunks of the passage at the

examiner. If you need to make longer references to the text, paraphrase (put it in your own words).
- In general, on Question 1, the IBO mark scheme awards 1 mark for each valid point made; ensure that your explanation is clear and reasonably full (whilst not overrunning in terms of time).

Question 2

- In answering questions that ask you to **evaluate** the **limitations** and **usefulness** of a particular source, focus on the source's origins (who produced it, when it was produced, etc), its purpose (why and for whom it was produced) and its content. Also, ensure that you identify both the source's value and limitations; otherwise, you will be unable to score more than a maximum of 2 marks for your answer.
- 'Value' means what the source is useful for, linked to its origin, purpose and content; 'limitation' means what aspects of the issue referred to in the question the source does *not* tell us about, and, the extent to which the source may not be reliable or accurate, linked to its origin, purpose and content.

Question 3

- In comparison questions, where you are asked to 'compare and contrast' two sources, do not forget to indicate both points of similarity and points of difference between the sources. If you only compared the two sources or only contrasted them, you could only gain a maximum of 4 out of 6 marks.
- You should make direct point-for-point comparison of the two sources and point-for-point contrast of the two sources.
- Do *not* deal with the two sources separately: you should *not* analyse the first source, then analyse the second source, and then briefly indicate where they are similar and where they differ.

Question 4

- In answering Question 4, which asks you to use **your own knowledge and the sources** to evaluate a particular area of the prescribed subject, the examiners will expect you to produce a short essay.
- I know that it is an obvious piece of advice, but do make sure that you use both the sources and your own knowledge; otherwise, you will lose marks (at least two sources must be used in your answer).
- In terms of approach, you will probably find it much more effective and time efficient to integrate the sources and your own knowledge, rather than running through what the sources have to contribute and then using your own knowledge. Equally, aim to take a thematic approach, using the sources and your own knowledge together, rather than going through each of the sources in turn.
- The mark scheme indicates that to get in to the top mark band (7–9 marks), an answer should synthesise the candidate's own knowledge with the sources.

HISTORY SL & HL: THE MOVE TO GLOBAL WAR

Using the Practice Questions in this Guide

Interspersed throughout both case studies (Japanese expansion in chapter 1; Italian and German expansion in chapter 2), I have included a number of practice Paper 1-style questions for you to practise on. These can be located using the index below.

List of Practice Questions

EXAM PRACTICE 1 6

EXAM PRACTICE 2 16

EXAM PRACTICE 3 26

EXAM PRACTICE 4 29

EXAM PRACTICE 5 40

EXAM PRACTICE 6 42

EXAM PRACTICE 7 45

EXAM PRACTICE 8 56

EXAM PRACTICE 9 65

EXAM PRACTICE 10 80

After each case study I have then also included suggested points for each of these questions.

In addition, at the end of each case study, I have created a complete set of practice Paper 1-style questions for you to practise on, with suggested points to incorporate in answering the questions and information relating to the Paper 1 mark-scheme.

The Syllabus for Prescribed Subject 3: The Move to Global War

Case Study 1: Japanese Expansion in East Asia (1931–1941)

Causes of expansion

- the impact of Japanese nationalism and militarism on foreign policy
- Japanese domestic issues: political and economic issues, and their impact on foreign relations
- political instability in China.

Events

- Japanese invasion of Manchuria and northern China (1931)
- Sino-Japanese War (1937–1941)
- the Three Power/Tripartite Pact; the outbreak of war; Pearl Harbor (1941).

Responses

- League of Nations and the Lytton Report
- political developments within China—the Second United Front
- international response, including US initiatives and increasing tensions between the US and Japan.

Case Study 2: German and Italian Expansion (1933–1940)

Causes of expansion

- impact of fascism and Nazism on the foreign policies of Italy and Germany
- impact of domestic economic issues on the foreign policies of Italy and Germany
- changing diplomatic alignments in Europe; the end of collective security; appeasement.

Events

- German challenges to the post-war settlements (1933–1938)
- Italian expansion: Abyssinia (1935-1936): Albania; entry into the Second World War
- German expansion (1938–1939); Pact of Steel, Nazi-Soviet Pact and the outbreak of war.

Responses

- international response to German aggression (1933–1938)
- international response to Italian aggression (1935–1936)
- international response to German and Italian aggression (1939–1940).

Chapter 1: Case Study: Japanese Expansion in East Asia (1931–1941)

1.1 Causes of Expansion

1.1.1 The Impact of Japanese Nationalism and Militarism on Foreign Policy

Up until the middle of the 19th century, Japan had been largely isolated from foreign influences. In theory, authority was vested in Japan's emperor but power was decentralised and exercised by an aristocracy of great lords (***daimyo***) and a caste of feudal warriors (***samurai***). Japan lacked natural resources and only 20% of its land was suitable for farming. Like China, Japan had not industrialised prior to the second half of the 19th century and, like China, Japan might have proved vulnerable to exploitation by the more advanced, industrialised western powers, which had stripped China of territory and extracted extensive economic concessions in the decades after the first **Opium War** (1839–1842). However, that did not prove to be the case. Instead, Japan, from the late 1860s, underwent rapid modernisation and, in the process, became the first industrialised Asian power.

> *"More isolated from the rest of the world than China before the arrival of an American squadron under Commodore Perry in 1853, the Japanese in less than two generations effected one of the most remarkable transformations of both government and economy that the world has ever seen. Whereas China acquired some of the appearance of a modern state—mostly in the form of western arms—Japan developed the substance."*
>
> C. J. Bartlett, *The Global Conflict*, p.27

Nationalism: pride in one's country; extreme nationalism can involve a feeling of superiority over other countries.

Militarism: the belief that a country should use force to promote its interests.

Daimyo: 'great names'—aristocratic lords in feudal Japan.

Samurai: feudal warrior class in medieval and early modern Japan.

Opium War (1839–42): a war fought between Britain and China, initiated by the British after the Qing Emperor confiscated opium that British merchants were bringing into China to sell illegally.

Full references are given in the bibliography at the end of this guide.

Modernisation

Japan's new leaders believed that Japan could only escape the fate of China by imitating western models of industrialisation and military, naval, educational and political modernisation. A popular slogan of this period in Japan was *'oitsuke, oikose'*—'catch up, overtake'; this expressed the view that Japan could only be made stronger by copying the western powers and then competing with them on equal terms. Consequently, Japanese officials and students were sent to Europe and the US in order to study western technology and economic and political structures, whilst western industrial, financial and military experts were brought to Japan to help oversee its modernisation; for example, in 1869 a naval academy was established in Japan, run mainly by British officers (Busch, p.112).

Why did Japan modernise?

1. **Because of the arrival of US warships under Commodore Perry in Japanese waters (1853)**

In 1854, Japan signed the Treaty of Kanagawa with the US, allowing US ships access to two Japanese ports and the establishment of a US Consulate in Japan. This soon paved the way for similar treaties with Britain, Russia and Holland. The foreign powers forced Japan to give up control over setting customs duties on their goods and foreigners were accorded the right of extraterritoriality, so that in the event of their breaking the law whilst in Japan, they would be tried by their own country's officials, rather than by the Japanese authorities. The Japanese widely resented these 'unequal' treaties, which fuelled a desire to strengthen Japan in order to prevent further western exploitation.

Figure 1.1: **Commodore Perry depicted in a Japanese woodblock**

2. **Japanese government dramatically changed with the so-called 'Meiji Restoration' (1868 onwards)**

This involved the abolition of the office of *shogun* by which Japan had been ruled since the twelfth century, and the restoration of real authority to the emperor. The *shogunate* was fatally undermined by its failure to protect Japan against foreign intervention in the 1860s.

Although the Meiji Restoration marked a shift of authority back to the emperor, power was now in practice principally wielded by a new ruling elite drawn initially from *samurai* (warrior) leaders who aimed to transform Japan into a modern industrial power, capable of resisting western interference.

Figure 1.2: **Emperor Meiji by Takahashi Yuichi**

Shogun: the office of supreme military commander who ruled medieval Japan in the name of the Emperor.

By 1875, the Japanese government employed over 500 foreigners. Tokyo University, founded in 1877, spent a third of its budget on salaries for foreign experts and lecturers (Kenneth G. Henshall, *A History of Japan*, 2012, p.79).

1871 saw the founding of the first national bank and a postal service and by 1872 the first railway line had been completed. By 1900, a network of 5,000 miles of track had been laid. The government saw the development of railways as the single most important prerequisite for modernisation and accordingly spent 33% of its expenditure on railway construction in the early/mid-1870s (Henshall, p.76).

1. CASE STUDY: JAPANESE EXPANSION IN EAST ASIA (1931–1941)

Industrialisation initially led by state investment but later by private investors

Much of Japan's initial industrialisation was driven by government investment. At the start of the **Meiji era**, Japan's more traditional businesses and merchants adopted a cautious approach to investment in new industries and technologies, with the government primarily—and, to a much lesser extent, entrepreneurs drawn from the lower ranking *samurai*—leading the way.

Meiji era: the period 1868–1912 when Japan was ruled by the Emperor Meiji.

Railway building in the 1870s was almost exclusively funded by the state but, by 1890, private investors carried out three-quarters (Henshall, p.94).

In 1880 the government sold off many of its industries, with the result that a few very large corporations, known as the '*zaibatsu*', emerged who owned a large proportion of the industrial and commercial sectors.

Zaibatsu: large Japanese business conglomerate.

Japanese industrialisation was spearheaded by textile industries, particularly silk. Later, from around the turn of the century, electrical goods industries developed rapidly, with NEC (Nippon Electric Company) set up in 1899 and Toshiba shortly afterwards. In the last decade and a half of the Meiji period, the government invested heavily in developing shipbuilding and set up the huge Yawata steel plant in 1901.

Japanese exports

By 1900, Japanese exports were worth approximately $200 million (Keylor, pp.14–15). Exports rose from around 6% of Japan's total **gross national product** (GNP) in the 1880s to about 20% by 1912. From the mid-1880s through to the First World War, Japan's total GNP grew by more than 3% each year. Whilst more than 50% of Japan's workers continued to be employed in agriculture, the contribution of agriculture to Japan's **gross domestic product (GDP)** fell from 42% (1885) to 31% (1912) (Henshall, p.95). The transformation of Japan's economy in the Meiji period (1868–1912) can be seen by the changing statistics for Japan's trade:

- In the 1870s, 91% of Japan's imports were manufactured goods.
- In the 1870s, most of Japan's exports were primary products; silk exports alone constituted 42% of the total.
- By 1914, 90% of Japan's exports were manufactured goods and more than 50% of its imports were primary products/raw materials (Henshall, p.96).

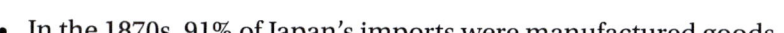
Gross national product (GNP): the total value of goods and services produced by the residents of a country.

Gross domestic product (GDP): GDP differs from GNP because GNP takes into account income receipts from abroad whereas GDP is a measure of national income and national output excluding income receipts from abroad.

Rapid urbanisation

Growing industrialisation and the revolution in transportation contributed to rapid **urbanisation**. Western dress was increasingly adopted by people living in Japanese towns and was made compulsory for officials from 1872 (Henshall, p.75–76). In the same year, the government announced that it aimed to provide education for all children and, by 1879, approximately two-thirds of boys and a quarter of girls were receiving primary school education (Henshall, p.80).

Urbanisation: growth of towns and cities.

Government and politics

Up until the Meiji Restoration, Japan had two 'capitals' in Edo and Kyoto. In 1868 the government moved to Edo, which was renamed Tokyo. Another major change involved the ending in 1871 of the feudal authority of the great territorial lords, the *daimyo*. A system of prefectures was established to replace the *daimyo*, by which Japan was divided up into a series of administrative units. The *samurai's* military authority was gradually ended as they were absorbed into the new Japanese Imperial Army and Navy, which from 1873 was organised on the Prussian model of universal male **conscription**.

Conscription: compulsory military service.

'Authoritarian democracy'

Japan also acquired a system of central government broadly based on western European lines with the creation of a cabinet and the promise of a national assembly—although, it was not until 1890 that the latter was set up. However, the state religion—*Shintoism*—emphasised the emperor's divine authority, which was in tension with the new liberal Japanese constitution, as indeed were other authoritarian tendencies such as the repressive conduct of the imperial police force, whose powers were increased by the **Peace Preservation Law** (1887) (Roberts, pp.62–63).

In fact, throughout the Meiji period, the Japanese state displayed a contradictory approach: on the one hand, some democratic reforms were introduced; but, on the other hand, repressive and authoritarian measures were adopted. Kenneth G. Henshall refers to this as 'authoritarian democracy', and as he puts it, the Japanese government felt that *"democracy…should be promoted, but in a controlled fashion and within limits."* (Henshall, p.82)

Growth of Japanese liberalism

Many educated Japanese were frustrated by the way in which a small group of politicians dominated Japan's government—they agitated for an end to this oligarchical rule and its replacement by a truly democratic system. This growing Japanese liberal movement resulted in the establishment in 1881 of the Liberal Party (*Jiyuto*), as Japan's first political party, followed in 1882 by the Constitutional Reform Party (*Rikken Kaishinto*). Both parties sought the broadening of political power and the introduction of a British-style constitution (Henshall, p.83).

Japan's oligarchs responded by making limited concessions, giving Japan the outward appearance of a democracy but not the substance and alternating between reform and authoritarianism. In 1875 government legislation severely restricted freedom of speech, but in 1879 a limited form of elected local government was introduced (Henshall, p.83).

The 1889 Constitution

Constitution: the rules under which a country is governed.

It was not until 1889 that Japan gained its first **constitution**, largely drafted by Ito Hirobumi, the dominant politician of the Meiji period. It was modelled on the Prussian or German constitution, rather than the British:

- The constitution established a two chamber Diet, with a House of Peers and an elected House of Representatives.
- Voting rights were restricted to men paying high levels of taxation, with the result that only around 2% of the adult population could vote.
- Cabinet ministers, as in Germany, were not responsible to the Diet but to the emperor himself.
- Similarly, the armed forces were accountable to the emperor, who was commander-in-chief.
- The constitution was presented as a gift from the emperor to his people and respect for the emperor's authority was at the core of it. However, the constitution did stipulate that all imperial decrees had to be counter-signed by a government minister.

1. CASE STUDY: JAPANESE EXPANSION IN EAST ASIA (1931–1941)

Kenneth G. Henshall's analysis of the new constitution's impact highlights the ambiguities of the new arrangements and how they allowed the oligarchs to retain their political power:

> *"The constitution was in some ways a step forward for democracy but one that still left the oligarchs, who acted in the name of the emperor, with the upper hand. It allowed the popular parties to have their say, but did not oblige the oligarchs to listen. It did not allow for effective party government.*
>
> Henshall, p.86.

Japanese politics were often highly unstable, with seven changes of Prime Minister between 1896 and 1901, although they were much more stable between 1901 and 1911.

Education and indoctrination

Increasingly the government tightened its control over education, in particular, dictating which books were to be used in schools. This control was used to inculcate **Confucian** and **Shinto** values and nationalism. In 1890, the government issued the *Imperial Rescript on Education*, which emphasised obedience to the state and to the emperor and which had to be memorised by all students.

Confucianism: a way of life taught by Confucius in China in the 6th–5th century BCE. It is primarily concerned with ethical principles.

Shinto: 'the way of the Gods'. It is an ancient religion based on the belief that spirits inhabit the natural world and involves rituals of nature worship.

What drove Japanese expansionism before the First World War?

1. **Shortage of raw materials**

   Japan had limited raw materials, so its economic development would potentially be hindered unless it was either able to pay for substantial imports and/or was able to gain raw materials through imperial expansion or acquisition of economic concessions in China.

2. **Demographic pressure**

   Japan, by 1900, had a large and rapidly increasing population. Japan's ruling elite reasoned that colonial expansion was required in order to relieve the demographic pressure on food resources and raw materials. Another reaction to population pressure was the beginning of mass migration by Japanese to other parts of Asia, the US, and Brazil.

   Demographic: relating to population.

3. **The desire to share in the scramble for China**

   During the nineteenth century China had been confronted by militarily and technologically superior powers such as Britain, France, the US, Germany, Russia, and Japan. They forced the Chinese to grant them trading bases and privileges and to admit Christian missionaries whose presence many Chinese resented.

   Foreign businessmen gained control of China's import and export trade and insisted that their trading bases be **extraterritorial**—not subject to the authority of Chinese laws. The chief ports, e.g. Shanghai, had large foreign-controlled districts. Foreign powers conquered outlying areas of the empire, e.g. Russia claimed Manchuria in 1900.

HISTORY SL & HL: THE MOVE TO GLOBAL WAR

EXAM PRACTICE 1

Source A: 'China—the cake of kings and...of emperors', French cartoon from January 1898; Source: Bibliotheque Nationale de France

Practice question:

For Question 1, part (b):

What is the message conveyed by Source A?   [2 marks]

Figure 1.3: "China – the cake of kings and... of Emperors"

The 1894–1895 Sino-Japanese War

In the 1890s, Japan joined in the grab for Chinese resources, with Korea and Manchuria its main objectives. Korea was a weak and divided kingdom, nominally owing homage to China, whilst Manchuria was part of the Chinese empire. Korea and Manchuria lay less than 70 kilometres to the west of Japan and, given China's weakness, presented a tempting prize to Japan's rulers. In 1876 Japan had forced Korea to grant it trade privileges.

In 1894 the King of Korea asked China for military help in dealing with a rebellion; China sent troops to Korea but Japan followed suit. China and Japan both refused to withdraw their troops from Korea and this stand-off led Japan to declare war on China in August 1894.

In the war of 1894–1895, Japan won a brilliant victory over China, showing its superiority in both land and naval forces. In the resulting Treaty of Shimonoseki (April 1895), Japan took Formosa (Taiwan) and the Liaodong Peninsula in southern Manchuria and obliged China to give up its interests in Korea, and to agree to pay a $25,000,000 indemnity. The victory and the subsequent peace settlement demonstrated the military and industrial progress that Japan had made since the 1860s.

Figure 1.4: **Japanese print of the Battle of the Yellow River (1894) by Korechika**

1. CASE STUDY: JAPANESE EXPANSION IN EAST ASIA (1931–1941)

The Tripartite Intervention: Japanese nationalism inflamed

However, Japanese nationalist feeling was incensed by the diplomatic intervention of Russia, France and Germany. Those three European powers, alarmed by Japan's crushing victory over China, jointly put pressure on Japan, in what became known as the **Tripartite Intervention**, to renounce some of the gains she had made under the Treaty of Shimonoseki. Japan was forced to give up the strategically important Liaodong peninsula and in 1896 accepted in the Yamagata-Lobanov protocol a joint protectorate with Russia over Korea.

Nationalist sentiment was further inflamed in 1898 when Russia forced China to grant it a 25-year lease on the Liaodong Peninsula.

The Tripartite Intervention: the diplomatic intervention of three countries (Russia, France and Germany) against Japan.

The Anglo-Japanese Alliance (1902)

Japan's victory in the 1884–1895 war with China earned Japan further respect from the western powers, who were already increasingly impressed by the modernisation achieved by Japan since the late 1860s. By 1897, the foreign powers had given up their rights of extraterritoriality in Japan and largely renounced their control over Japanese tariffs. Further confirmation of Japan's growing status was the signing of an alliance with Britain in 1902, under the terms of which each was obliged to help the other if it found itself at war with more than one country and to remain neutral if the other went to war with one other country.

The Russo-Japanese War (1904–1905)

Blocked in the Balkans (South-Eastern Europe) since the **Congress of Berlin (1878)**, Russia turned to the Far East, encouraged by the weakness of the Chinese Empire. In 1898, the Chinese government allowed Russia to build a railway across Manchuria and granted it a 25-year lease on the Liaodong Peninsula, including Port Arthur. At this point a number of Tsar Nicholas II's ministers urged him to look to expand into Korea too. This brought Russia into conflict with Japan, which regarded Korea as its sphere of influence. In Japan, in 1901, nationalists set up the Amur River Society, an organisation committed to promoting Japanese imperialist expansion. The Amur River Society attracted a lot of support within Japan's armed forces. Since 1897 the Japanese government had spent over half of its annual budget on the military, creating powerful land and naval forces.

Figure 1.5: **Map of the battlefields of the Russo-Japanese War**

Congress of Berlin (1878): an international conference held in Berlin after the Russian-Turkish War of 1877–78 ended.

Negotiations between Russia and Japan broke down in February 1904.

August 1904:	Japan attacked Russia's naval base in Manchuria, Port Arthur.
January 1905:	Port Arthur surrendered to the Japanese.
March 1905:	Japanese forces took Mukden, the capital of Manchuria.
May 1905:	Russia's Baltic fleet, having sailed half way across the world, was destroyed at the Tsushima Straits.
September 1905:	Russia agreed peace terms with Japan in the Treaty of Portsmouth (US), in which President Roosevelt of the US acted as a mediator; Russia had to agree to withdraw from Manchuria and hand over its lease on the Liaodong Peninsula to Japan, as well as the southern half of Sakhalin Island.

Japan's victory in the war with Russia earned it great respect internationally, as J. M. Roberts notes:

> The Battle of Tsushima "ensured Japanese victory in the first defeat of a European power by non-Europeans in a major war since the Middle Ages. The moral, political and strategic repercussions were immense."
>
> (Roberts, p.213)

Despite growing international recognition of Japan's status as a power, once again Japanese nationalists, as with the treaty following the 1894–1895 war with China, were deeply unhappy with the Treaty of Portsmouth, particularly the failure to extract an **indemnity** from Russia, and serious rioting broke out in Tokyo and other major cities. Martial law had to be imposed and Prime Minister Katsura resigned.

Indemnity: a financial penalty.

In the years following its victory over Russia, Japan steadily expanded its control over Korea, brutally suppressing Korean resistance until, in 1910, it annexed Korea and incorporated it in to the Japanese empire.

The Taisho Era (1912–1926)

The Meiji emperor died in 1912 and his successor took the name 'Taisho.' During the Taisho Era, the authority of the *Genro* came to an end and modern political parties began to acquire greater influence. However, just before the advent of the Taisho era, the creation of the Special Higher Police Force in 1911, tasked with repressing left-wing political activists, highlighted the ongoing tension between authoritarianism and democracy within Japanese politics.

Genro: the group of older statesmen who had guided Japan's government through the Meiji period.

Japan and the First World War (1914–1918)

Soon after the outbreak of the First World War, Japan declared war on Germany and seized Qingdao, a German concession in northern China, the railway running from Qingdao to Jinan in Shandong, and several German-owned Pacific islands.

The Twenty-One Demands (January 1915)

Japan issued the **Twenty-One Demands** to the Chinese government, requiring it to agree to:

- extend Japan's lease on Port Arthur and the South Manchuria Railway
- recognise Japan's dominant position in Shandong

- employ Japanese political and military advisers and have a joint Chinese-Japanese police force.

Britain and the US protested at Japan's demands for the appointment of political and military advisers and for a joint Chinese-Japanese police force, so Japan announced it would postpone those particular demands. On 25 May 1915, China's President, Yuan Shi-kai, accepted Japan's demands, sparking widespread anti-Japanese demonstrations and boycotts of Japanese goods in China.

Japan was able to exploit the First World War to its considerable benefit, in economic, territorial and diplomatic terms.

The diplomatic impact of the First World War on Japan

Japan's enhanced international influence is evidenced by the significant place it was accorded in the peace negotiations at Paris in 1919 and at the **Washington Naval Conference** in 1921–1922. Japan's acquisition of Germany's former **concession** in Shandong from China, and of German's former Pacific colonies, was confirmed by the **Versailles Treaty**, although Shandong was soon returned to China. Furthermore, Japan was given a permanent seat on the Council of the newly-established **League of Nations**.

However, Japan was deeply angered by the rejection of its proposed racial equality clause for inclusion in the League of Nations' Covenant (its charter).

Washington Naval Conference: an international conference held in order to prevent a naval arms race in the Pacific.

Concession: trading rights and other privileges.

Versailles Treaty: the treaty imposed on Germany at the end of the First World War.

League of Nations: an international peacekeeping organisation set up in 1919.

Ambivalent Japanese attitudes towards the West

Much of the Japanese elite in the 1920s saw co-operation with Europe and the US as the way to best serve Japan's interests, but other influential groups in Japan regarded the West with suspicion, resented what they saw as the West's racial prejudice towards the Asiatic races and believed that Japan should turn its back on western culture and return to more traditional ways. The hand of such Japanese nationalists was strengthened by the outraged reaction within Japan to the US's Immigration Act (1924), which, in tightening up on immigration into the US, singled out Japanese immigrants and effectively banned them altogether. Prior to this, there had been large-scale Japanese migration to the US.

The economic impact of the First World War on Japan

Japan's GNP rose by a staggering 40% during the First World War. The First World War had a massive impact on the pattern of international trade as the US exploited Britain, France and Germany's concentration on the production of war goods to expand its commercial penetration of Latin America, whilst Japan benefitted enormously in increasing its trade in Asia at Britain, Germany and France's expense.

As William R. Keylor puts it:

> *"From an economic point of view, the First World War was won by the United States and Japan, both of which avoided territorial destruction or loss of life on a large scale while acquiring economic predominance within their respective geographic regions."*
>
> Keylor, p 105

This shift in the economic balance of power is confirmed by the following statistics:

- In the period 1913–1929, the total value of world exports rose by two-thirds.
- Britain's exports increased by just 15% and Germany's by 33%, whilst Japan's trebled.

Japanese foreign policy (1919–1930)

Although Japan had been an expansionist power since the late 19th century, taking advantage of China's weakness to extract concessions and take territory from it—notably, Taiwan and, following their victory over Russia in 1905, Korea—in the period 1919–1930, the Japanese government largely pursued a conciliatory policy towards the US, the European powers and China.

Up until 1931, Japan, most of the time, co-operated with the West:

- Japan signed the Washington Naval Treaty in 1922, which meant Japan accepting a position of naval inferiority compared to Britain and the US.
- Japan played a significant role in the League of Nations, as a permanent member of the Council.
- Japan also benefitted from close economic and financial ties with the US and the European powers.
- This was also true of Japan's relations with China in the 1920s; Baron Shidehara Kijuro, Japan's foreign minister for much of the period 1924–1931, favoured a conciliatory policy towards China, which was the destination of 25% of Japanese exports in the 1920s.

Figure 1.6: **Foreign Minister Shidehara**

As the historian C. J. Bartlett observes:

> "The Washington settlement of 1921–22 had worked fairly well in the 1920s, and superficially it appeared to be reaffirmed and even extended at the London Naval Conference in 1930. From 1921 the majority of the Japanese ruling elite, with varying degrees of enthusiasm, had attempted to work broadly within Anglo-Saxon conceptions of world order."
>
> Bartlett, p 147

1.1.2 Japanese Domestic Issues: Political and Economic Issues, and Their Impact on Foreign Relations

From 1931 onwards, Japanese foreign policy became more aggressive and brought it into conflict to varying degrees with China, the USSR, the US, France and Great Britain.

Why did Japanese foreign policy become more aggressive after 1931?

1. **The rise of authoritarian politics in Japan**

    One factor propelling Japan's increasingly aggressive foreign policy was the move towards a more authoritarian system of politics, in which the military exerted growing influence. Up until 1931, Japanese politics were characterised by the same contradictory currents of authoritarianism and democracy that we have noted in the late Meiji era. The main political parties gained greater representation in the Cabinet, but Japanese governments never represented, to the same extent, the outcome of an election in the way that was true in democratic states such as Britain and France. The closest Japan got to this was in 1918–1921, under Takashi's premiership, but subsequent cabinets were non-party based in their makeup and represented powerful political and business oligarchs.

1. CASE STUDY: JAPANESE EXPANSION IN EAST ASIA (1931–1941)

The year 1925 clearly highlights the ambiguities within the Japan political system:

On the one hand, The Peace Preservation Law made it illegal to promote changes to Japan's political and constitutional framework; whilst, on the other, universal male **suffrage** was introduced for all men aged 25 and over.

Suffrage: the right to vote

From 1931 onwards, the ambiguities within Japanese politics began to be resolved in favour of an increasingly authoritarian and military-dominated political climate. This trend was powerfully driven by the impact of the **Wall Street Crash** and **Great Depression**, from October 1929 onwards, but it was also set in motion by growing economic difficulties that predated the Wall Street Crash.

Wall Street Crash: the catastrophic fall in share prices on the New York Stock Exchange in October 1929.

Great Depression: the term given to the huge economic downturn in the USA which affected most of the world in the early and mid-1930s.

2. **The growth of aggressive nationalism in Japan in the 1930s**

   Although the First World War had stimulated tremendous economic growth in Japan, the post-war period saw a widening gap between the wealth of the gigantic *zaibatsu* and smaller businesses.

   Japan's economy soon went into a long-term recession:

   - 1927 saw a severe financial crisis in which 25% of Japan's banks collapsed.
   - Japanese society and Japan's economy both came under severe pressure from rapid urbanisation in the first 30 years of the 20th century. Japan's population increased from 42 million in 1895 to over 70 million by 1933, with the urban population rising from 12% of the total population to 45%.

   Japanese farmers, as elsewhere in the world, were hit by falling agricultural produce prices, with rural incomes being reduced by two-thirds between 1926 and 1931 (Henshall, p 108). Rural hardship helped fuel aggressive nationalism in Japan as rural communities tended to be more conservative and less internationally-minded in their attitudes. Furthermore, the bulk of recruits to Japan's armed forces were drawn from the countryside, helping shape the generally nationalistic outlook of the military.

   Both in rural and urban communities from the mid-1920s onwards, the economic downturn, soon to become an economic disaster when Wall Street crashed in the US in 1929, led increasing numbers of Japanese to blame western influences for their problems, and, to reject as corrupt, parliamentary institutions, big business and **western individualism**. The growth of aggressive nationalism was evident in 1930 in the hostile reaction of many Japanese to the London Naval Conference's failure to give Japan a higher ratio of ships than that permitted by the Washington Treaty. One extreme nationalist shot Japan's Prime Minister, Hamaguchi Osachi, in protest at the government's alleged weakness in negotiating with the US and Great Britain. Hamaguchi died of his wounds the following year.

   Western individualism: emphasis in western culture on the interests and rights of the individual.

3. **The impact of the Great Depression on Japan**

   The Wall Street Crash created an unprecedented economic crisis in Japan, leading to a dramatic change in its foreign policy, an increasingly authoritarian style of politics and the growing political influence of Japan's armed forces.

   - Unemployment reached 2.6 million in 1930.
   - Exports fell by almost 50% in the period 1929–1931.
   - By 1932, the price of silk fell to 20% of its 1923 figure. Half of Japan's farmers were dependent on silk and blamed the government for their plight.

HISTORY SL & HL: THE MOVE TO GLOBAL WAR

Many Japanese, particularly in the armed forces, turned their back on co-operation with the West and with China, and saw imperialist aggression as a way out of Japan's economic difficulties. Starting with the invasion of Manchuria in 1931, Japan embarked on an aggressive foreign policy, which challenged the West and disrupted the international order. This course was ultimately to lead Japan to the full-scale invasion of China in 1937, the occupation of **Indo-China** in 1940, and the attack on Pearl Harbor in 1941.

Indo-China: name by which France's colonial possessions in South-East Asia, comprising Vietnam, Cambodia and Laos, were collectively known.

The failure of democracies like the US and Britain to prevent the onset of the Great Depression discredited democracy in the eyes of many Japanese and facilitated the growth of aggressive nationalism in Japan. Many Japanese nationalists admired the way that Hitler restored economic growth and full employment in Germany.

Keynesian: economic ideas relating to stimulating growth put forward by John Maynard Keynes.

In fact, the Japanese government responded boldly to the economic crisis by adopting radical **Keynesian** principles, hugely increasing government investment, and, this seems to have been the key factor in Japan recovering more quickly from the impact of the Great Depression than many other countries. Between 1936 and 1940, Japan's economy grew at an average of 5% a year (Henshall, p.115). However, by the time the Japanese economy began to recover, Japan's domestic and foreign politics had been channelled into an increasingly authoritarian and aggressive direction.

4. **The growth of militarism in Japan**

Following the dramatic downturn in the Japanese economy, many Japanese nationalists, particularly in the armed forces, saw Manchuria as a tempting prize because it was a vast region, rich in mineral resources, and Japan already had economic concessions there and troops stationed there and nearby in Korea. Since the 1904–1905 Russo-Japanese War, Japan had control of Korea (which bordered Manchuria) and annexed it in 1910. By the late 1920s, Japan controlled part of the Liaodong Peninsula on the south coast of Manchuria and the South Manchurian Railway.

1.1.3 Political Instability in China

The Chinese Empire suffered a series of military defeats in the 19th century, which led to foreign countries exploiting it. This foreign domination undermined the ruling Qing dynasty and encouraged the development of nationalist movements. In 1911, revolution swept away the Qing and China became a republic, but this ushered in a period of weak government and civil war, known as the 'Warlord Era' (1916–27). During this period, the Beijing government never controlled more than a fraction of China as regional **warlords** ran different areas of the country.

Warlords: generals from the former imperial army who competed for power after 1911.

Guomindang (GMD): known also as the Nationalists, the party was founded by Sun Yat-sen after China became a republic in 1912.

The emergence of Nationalist China

In 1926–1927 the **Guomindang (GMD)** party launched the Northern Expedition, aimed at defeating the warlords and creating an effective national government for the whole of China. The expedition was led by Chiang Kai-shek (Jiang Jieshi) and, by the end of 1927, he had established a new Nationalist government based in Nanjing.

There are two systems of transliterating Chinese characters into English. Most textbooks now use the more modern Pinyin version but some still use the older Wade-Giles system. I have largely used the Pinyin version but for some names, e.g. Chiang Kai-shek, have used the Wade-Giles version as opposed to the Pinyin (Jiang Jieshi). Do not worry about which version you use—both are acceptable.

1. CASE STUDY: JAPANESE EXPANSION IN EAST ASIA (1931–1941)

Japanese aggression from 1931 onwards can be seen as a response to this changing political situation in China, which appeared to threaten Japanese interests. The Japanese became worried that Chiang Kai-shek's Nationalist government might try to end Japan's concessions in Manchuria because the Nationalists were demanding an end to all foreign concessions in China. Furthermore, Manchuria was proving an increasingly volatile region with the warlord running Manchuria, Zhang Xueliang, seeking to eliminate foreign influences there. Japanese officers had assassinated Zhang's father, Zhang Zuolin, in June 1928, blowing his train up, in an apparent attempt to justify a Japanese military takeover of Manchuria. However, on this occasion, senior commanders in the Japanese military intervened to prevent events escalating.

In 1929, Zhang seized Soviet assets and citizens in Manchuria. This provoked a Soviet military response in November in which a single division of the Red Army forced 30,000 of Zhang's troops to retreat. A truce was arranged in December, but the Japanese would have noted the weakness of Zhang's troops and the lack of a response from either Chiang Kai-shek or the international community (Tohmatsu and Willmott, p 26).

1.2 *EVENTS:* The Japanese Invasion of Manchuria and Northern China (1931)

The Mukden Incident (September 1931)

In September 1931, the Japanese army in Manchuria, known as the **Kwantung Army,** occupied much of Manchuria. This was after it had staged the Mukden Incident, blowing up part of the South Manchurian Railway, just north of Mukden, and blaming it on the Chinese. Many Japanese nationalists, particularly within the armed forces, saw Manchuria as a tempting prize for the reasons discussed above. Moreover, they feared that, unless they took action to secure Japanese interests in Manchuria, Chiang Kai-shek and/or Zhang Xueliang would seek to force the Japanese to relinquish their assets and concessions in the region.

Kwantung Army: the name by which Japanese military forces guarding Japanese assets in Manchuria, including the South Manchurian Railway, were known.

The takeover of Manchuria was a decision taken by Kwantung army officers stationed in Manchuria, led by Lieutenant-Colonel Ishiwara Kanji, with the backing of some senior military figures in Tokyo; the Japanese government, however, did not authorise it and sought to limit the Kwantung army's intervention. The army ignored the Japanese government's protests and came to exert an increasing influence over the government. Prime Minister Wakatsuki Reijiro resigned, having failed to control the military. His successor, Inukai Tsuyoshi, was assassinated by naval officers in 1932, after he tried to restrain Japan's armed forces in Manchuria.

The Kwantung army was able to take over most of Manchuria easily by November 1931 as Zhang Xueliang complied with Chiang Kai-shek's orders to withdraw his troops south rather than engage the Kwantung army. However, Japanese offensives in Manchuria were not concluded until November 1932.

The Shanghai Incident (January 1932)

Fighting between Japanese and Chinese forces escalated briefly in January 1932 when skirmishes broke out in Shanghai between Chinese troops and Japanese marines who were protecting Japanese citizens and property in the international quarter. The Japanese subjected Shanghai to aerial bombing. In May, the Japanese withdrew from Shanghai after agreeing a truce with the Chinese authorities.

The establishment of Manchukuo (February 1932)

The Japanese proclaimed the new state of Manchukuo, claiming it was an independent country. Japan placed Pu Yi, the last Chinese emperor who had abdicated in 1912, on the throne as a **puppet ruler**.

Puppet ruler: a ruler with no real power, under the control of others

1.2.1 RESPONSES: The League of Nations and the Lytton Report

The League responded slowly and ineffectually to the Japanese occupation of Manchuria. This was partly because the situation in Manchuria was so complex given the unstable nature of China since the 1911 Revolution; the Chinese government's control over Manchuria had been limited prior to the Japanese occupation and Japan had had a presence there since the 1905 war with Russia. Furthermore, the European powers were not very sympathetic to the Chinese leader, Chiang Kai-shek, because he was seeking to end foreign concessions in China.

There were many reasons why the League took a soft line against Japan, including its members' preoccupation with the Great Depression and the strong military force that Japan's Kwantung Army constituted. The effects of the absence of great powers, notably the US and the USSR, were graphically demonstrated in the Manchurian Crisis. In responding to Japan's occupation of Manchuria, the League decided neither to impose economic nor military sanctions on Japan. The League's leading powers, Britain and France, reasoned that neither would be effective without the US's support (they were the greatest financial and military power in the region), and they were worried that any attempt to impose sanctions might provoke a Japanese attack on their colonies in the Far East.

Stanley Baldwin, a minister in the British cabinet, put this very clearly in February 1932:

Economic boycott: the cutting off of trade

> *"If you enforce an economic boycott you'll have war declared by Japan and she will seize Singapore and Hong Kong, and we can't, as we are placed, stop her. You'll get nothing out of Washington but words, big words, but only words."*
>
> Quoted in Fry, p 97

October 1931: Japan blocked the Council's resolution	China initially appealed to the League under Article 11 of the Covenant; under Article 11, a Council member that was involved in a dispute could veto a Council resolution. This is precisely what happened in late October 1931; Japan vetoed the Council resolution calling on her to withdraw her forces to the area around the South Manchuria Railway. Japan, probably hoping to buy time, proposed a commission of inquiry into the Mukden Incident.
December 1931: The League voted to set up the Lytton Commission	The Council accordingly voted to set up the Lytton Commission to investigate the Mukden Incident. The **Lytton Commission**, led by the English aristocrat, Lord Lytton, spent April–June 1932 in Manchuria doing so.
March 1932: China appealed to the League Assembly using Article 15	The British hoped that, through the League, a formula regarding Manchuria's status acceptable to both China and Japan could be found. In February–March 1932, the League of Nations passed resolutions that members of the League should not recognise changes in the status of territory resulting from the use of force.

1. CASE STUDY: JAPANESE EXPANSION IN EAST ASIA (1931–1941)

October 1932: The Lytton Report published	It was not until October 1932 that the Lytton Report was published; it recommended that Manchuria should be an autonomous state but still under Chinese **sovereignty**.	
February 1933: The League Assembly upheld the Lytton Report	The League took until February 1933 to vote to accept the report. Instead of trying to force Japan out of Manchuria, the League opted for a policy of 'non-recognition'—refusing to recognise Manchukuo as an independent state, which Japan claimed it now was. Japan promptly walked out of the League.	 Figure 1.7: **The Lytton Commission inspecting the South Manchurian railway line**
The US's response	The American government was divided over how to respond to Japan's invasion; Secretary of State, Henry Stimson, favoured a tough stance, possibly involving economic sanctions, but he was overruled by President Hoover who decided on a policy of US non-recognition of the new puppet state of Manchukuo. The so-called 'Stimson Non-Recognition Doctrine' was announced in January 1932.	

Sovereignty: ownership/ultimate authority

Stimson Non-Recognition Doctrine: the USA's official refusal to recognise Manchukuo as an independent country. Henry Stimson was US Secretary of State in 1929–32.

Why did the League fail to prevent the Japanese takeover of Manchuria?

1. The two greatest military powers in the region—the US and the USSR—were not members of the League.
2. It fell to Britain and France to lead the League against Japan's aggression. However, both were aware of the vulnerability of their colonial holdings in the Far East and were not even keen on imposing sanctions.
3. The League's procedures were slow and this contributed to the delay in deciding on a response to Japan's invasion. This was compounded by China's appeal under Article 11 (see above), which meant that Japan was able to veto the Council's resolution calling on the withdrawal of Japanese troops to the railway zone.
4. To an extent, British and French politicians were not unsympathetic to increased Japanese control of Manchuria because Japan had already considerable influence and concessions there and because China was still in a very unstable situation. Furthermore, for Britain, there were not enough in the way of British commercial and financial interests in China for the British government to risk a major confrontation with Japan; China took only 2.5% of Britain's exports and accounted for just 5% of British foreign investment.
5. Britain and France were preoccupied with the effects of the Great Depression on their countries; the financial crisis peaked in 1931 with numerous banks collapsing.

Source B: Anthony P. Adamthwaite summarises the reasons for the League's failure over Manchuria:

> Manchuria demonstrated that the League was toothless. Collective security depended on the readiness of the great powers to defend the status quo. Although Britain, France and the United States had much to lose in the Far East, Japanese expansion was not yet seen as a direct threat to western commercial and colonial interests. Indeed, France was inclined to see Japan as a bastion of order against anarchy and **Bolshevism**. In fact, there was no chance of collective action against Japan. Western governments were engrossed in problems of economic recovery and disarmament negotiations (Adamthwaite, p.37).

Bolshevism: Russian communism.

Practice question

For Question 1, part (a):

Why according to Source B did the League of Nations fail to stop Japan's takeover of Manchuria? [3 marks]

The Manchurian Crisis soured relations between Japan, on the one hand, and, Britain, France and the US, on the other. Although Britain and France's response to Japan's aggression was very limited, going no further than supporting the League of Nations' condemnation of Japan and refusing to recognise the puppet state of Manchukuo set up by the Japanese, it was enough to lead Japanese nationalists to feel offended and ostracised by the international community. This was illustrated by Japan's decision to walk out of the League of Nations.

The US's Neutrality Acts

- In 1935, the US Senate passed a provisional Neutrality Act.
- This was followed in 1937 by a full Neutrality Act, which committed the US government to neutrality in the event of future wars between foreign countries.

Neutrality: not supporting either side in a conflict.

The US's reluctance to involve itself in international crises in the 1930s in part explains the weak stance taken by Britain and France in dealing with acts of aggression by Japan, as well as by Germany and Italy.

1.3   *EVENTS:* Sino-Japanese War (1937–1941)

The domestic context for growing Japanese aggression

Domestic politics in Japan: the growing influence of the military and of militarism in Japan

Domestic: the internal affairs of a state.

The takeover of Manchuria marked a key moment in the shift of power from civilian politicians to the military. The decision had been taken by Kwantung army officers, with the backing of some senior military figures in Tokyo; the Japanese government had not authorised it and the army ignored the Japanese government's protests. In the **15 May Incident (1932)**, nationalist officers assassinated Prime Minister Inukai who had been

1. CASE STUDY: JAPANESE EXPANSION IN EAST ASIA (1931–1941)

trying to reach a solution to the Manchurian crisis that would leave China with some semblance of sovereignty over Manchuria.

'Government by assassination'

Inukai was Japan's last Prime Minister to be drawn from a leading parliamentary political party. Historians are unsure about what Emperor Hirohito thought about the army's takeover of Manchuria, but he took no action and made no public comment, despite his brother Prince Chichibu urging him to intervene to restrain the military (Henshall, p.110).

From May 1932 onwards, *"governments could only be made with the assent of the military and only if they were prepared to accept the military's demands"* (Tohmatsu and Willmott, p.38). The period 1932–1941 saw ten different administrations in power as Japanese politics became highly unstable. Ministers, such as the former Finance Minister, Inoue Junnosuke, who pursued policies at odds with the Japanese military, were assassinated. Violent interventions by ultra-nationalists within the military reached their bloodiest in the **February 26 Incident** in 1936.

February 26 Incident: a large scale attempted military coup in 1936 which was put down by troops who remained loyal to the government.

Military factions

Although the military's increasing influence in Japan's political system is very clear, it needs to be pointed out that the armed forces were not united in their outlook and actually contained a variety of factions:

- **The Imperial Way Faction** (*Kodo-ha*), which favoured war with the USSR, and instigated the Mukden Incident
- **The Control Faction** (*Tosei-ha*), which favoured expansion into China and consisted of more senior, less radical officers. The Imperial Way Faction was eventually brought under control in 1936 by the Control Faction, following an attempted military coup by the Imperial Way. The coup involved 1,400 troops and several political leaders were assassinated. In a rare political intervention, Emperor Hirohito, condemned the February 26 Incident and ensured that the ring leaders of the attempted coup were tried for treason.

Figure 1.8: **Japanese rebels in the February 26 mutiny**

Despite the failure of the extremists within the Imperial Way to install a military government, the aftermath of the February 26 Incident saw the military's influence over the government hugely increased by the new Prime Minister, Koki Hirota, who was appointed just after the **abortive coup**. Koki Hirota introduced a much larger military budget, increased government investment in war-related industries, and reintroduced the principle that army and navy ministers could only be appointed from among serving military commanders (Henshall, p.117).

Abortive coup: a failed attempt to seize power by force.

The 'civilian-military split' thesis

After the Second World War, the International Military Tribunal for the Far East was set up to prosecute Japanese 'war criminals.' The prosecution argued that the Manchurian Crisis marked the point at which a **'militaristic clique'** took control of government in

Militaristic clique: A military faction

Japan and forced a fundamental change in foreign policy away from co-operation with the West, putting Japan on an imperialist path to war. Many historians have taken the same approach to Japanese history in this period, seeing the period 1931–45 as one of a piece wherein ultra-nationalist extremists in the armed forces hijacked control of the state and directed it towards a succession of wars of expansion.

The challenge to the 'civilian-military split' thesis

James Crowley and Michael Barnhart have convincingly challenged this 'civilian-military split' thesis recently. They argue that Japanese expansionism can be seen as a rational response to economic and strategic threats facing Japan in the 1930s—such as Nationalist China's determination to end foreign concessions in China, the impact of the Great Depression, and the growing power of the USSR. Furthermore, they suggest that an increasingly aggressive foreign policy after 1931 was favoured not just by extremists in the armed forces but also by civilian politicians.

The growth of ultra-nationalism

The growth in ultra-nationalist politics was encouraged by the Ministry of Education's publication in March 1937 of the *Cardinal Principles of the Nation*, which ordered schools and universities to use with their students. This book promoted the idea of the **divinity** of the emperor and the obligation of loyal Japanese to devote themselves to service to the emperor and nation. By the mid-1930s, new textbooks for primary school children had increasingly military and nationalistic themes and tones.

Divinity: god-like nature

Figure 1.9: **The Emperor Hirohito at his coronation in 1928**

The historians Haruo Tohmatsu and H. P. Willmott see the Japanese press's extravagant praise in 1932 for a Japanese officer who killed himself because he felt shame in being taken prisoner in fighting in Shanghai, after being badly wounded, as indicative of a significant shift in societal attitudes. They contrast this with the fact that thousands of Japanese soldiers were taken prisoner during the war with Russia in 1904–1905 and were not treated with disrespect when they returned home, many receiving medals for bravery (Tohmatsu and Willmott, p.16). Tohmatsu and Willmott argue that the Manchurian Incident facilitated the emergence of *"a harsher form of nationalism to find expression within Japan."* (Tohmatsu and Willmott, p.17)

The 1930s also saw the growing popularity of the view that Japan had a special destiny to liberate Asia from western domination and to create a united Asia, led by Japan. Tatsuo Kawai was particularly influential in promoting this vision of an Asia united under Japan leadership and dominated by it, publishing *The Goal of Japanese Expansion* in 1938.

1. CASE STUDY: JAPANESE EXPANSION IN EAST ASIA (1931–1941)

Louise Young points out that the advent of mass politics in Japan in the 1920s altered *"the process of imperial policy-making in Japan"*:

> *"Thus, whether army officers are to be held accountable for an irrational war or commended for trying to make the best of a bad set of choices, they must share either the censure or the accolades with the wide variety of interest groups that helped mobilize popular support for the advance into China and south-east Asia. This included the mass media as well as academic institutions, women's and youth groups, chambers of commerce…and a host of other institutions."*
>
> Louise Young, 1999, p.174

Japanese expansion (1933–1937)

Before examining the Sino-Japanese War of 1937–1941, it is worth noting some further **historiographical debates** surrounding the origins of the war. Historians, such as John Boyle, treat the **Manchurian Incident (1931–1933)** and the **China Incident of 1937** as separate conflicts. However, others, notably Louise Young, regard the two conflicts as inextricably linked:

> *"And yet, the facility with which Japan occupied Manchuria nurtured the hubris of Japanese ambitions to crush the Nationalists [Chinese] in a quick and decisive strike, and fed mounting ambitions to absorb all of China's vast territories."*
>
> Young, p.167

Historiographical debates: differing interpretations put forward by historians.

Manchurian Incident (1931–33): the Japanese army's takeover of Manchuria.

China Incident (1937): the term by which Japan referred to the opening stages of the Sino-Japanese War of 1937–45. The Japanese avoided using the term 'war' because they wanted to deter international intervention.

Indeed, in looking at Japan's expansion in to northern China and Inner Mongolia in the period 1933–1937, it is clear that, having successfully taken control of Manchuria, Japanese nationalists were encouraged to press for further aggression against China. This was partly because Chiang Kai-shek put up little resistance to the Japanese takeover of Manchuria.

Japan takes Jehol

Further Japanese expansion in to northern China followed, with a major offensive in Jehol Province, to the south of Manchuria, in February–March 1933. Chiang Kai-shek (Jiang Jieshi) eventually was prepared to sign the **Tanggu Truce** with Japan (May 1933). Chiang's passive response was partly because his first priority was to defeat his internal enemies, the Communists, and unify the country, and partly because he recognised that his forces were inferior to Japan's armed forces. Chiang agreed to full restoration of diplomatic relations with Japan in June 1935.

Tanggu Truce: a ceasefire agreement, signed at Tanggu in northern China by Japan and the Guomindang government, which formally ended the Manchurian Crisis.

Japan takes over Inner Mongolia

However, Chiang's weak response emboldened Japan to further aggression; by 1937, Japan had extended its control to Inner Mongolia. Japan's growing imperialist ambitions were made clear by the Amau Declaration in April 1934 and its indication that it intended to embark on a major naval construction programme.

The Amau Declaration (April 1934)

The Japanese foreign ministry issued a statement in which it declared that Japan would exercise a **protectorate** over China and take on the role of *"guardian of peace and order in eastern Asia"* (Tohmatsu and Willmott, p.16). This was followed a few months later by the Japanese government's announcement in December that, once the Washington Naval Treaty expired in 1936, it would renounce the naval limitations that it had signed up to as part of that agreement.

The London Naval Conference (1935–1936)

The **London Naval Conference** strengthened Japanese nationalists in their conviction that the western powers would not accept Japan as an equal and that therefore Japan should abandon international co-operation, and, instead, promote Japanese interests through imperial expansion. Japan had insisted on equality with the US and Britain in terms of ratios of fleets and left the conference when the US and Britain refused to concede this.

The growing influence of anti-democratic, ultra-nationalist elements within the Japanese government can also be seen in Japan's signing of the **Anti-Comintern Pact** in November 1936 with Germany in which they agreed to co-operate in combatting the spread of communism.

Anti-Comintern Pact: an agreement originally signed by Germany and Japan, promising to co-operate in stopping the spread of communism.

The outbreak of the Sino-Japanese War (July 1937)

The war was initiated by the **Marco Polo Bridge Incident** on 7 July 1937 in which Japanese and Chinese patrols exchanged fire just outside Beijing. In August, fighting spread to Shanghai, and, by October 1937, Japan had sent 15 army divisions to China (Tohmatsu and Willmott, p.16).

Phase one (1937–1938)

The first phase of the war lasted until October 1938 and saw large-scale Japanese offensives in northern and central China. The Japanese pushed south from Manchuria and Jehol and made landings on the east coast. Nationalist forces initially fought bravely, but they were driven out of the lower Yangzi Valley by superior Japanese forces.

Nanjing: a city located in the lower Yangtze River region in China, known under the older Wade-Giles transliteration system as Nanking.

November 1937:	Shanghai fell.
December 1937:	**The Rape of Nanjing**—the Japanese took Nanjing, killing 200,000–300,000 Chinese civilians. The Japanese mistakenly believed that the fall of Nanjing would lead Chiang to seek peace terms but instead the Nationalists retreated westwards beyond the mountains of Sichuan province, opening the dikes on the Yellow River in June 1938 in order to slow down the Japanese; at least 500,000 Chinese drowned.

Figure 1.10: **Japanese troops entering Nanjing**

1. CASE STUDY: JAPANESE EXPANSION IN EAST ASIA (1931–1941)

October 1938:
: The Nationalists had moved their capital to Wuhan but this fell to the Japanese in October 1938 and shortly afterwards Chiang established his new base at Chongqing (Chungking) in the western province of Sichuan, on the upper Yangzi, where the Japanese proved unable to break through the mountains protecting Chongqing.

: The Japanese captured China's last major port, Guangzhou (Canton), which severely limited the Nationalists' ability to bring in supplies from abroad.

: The positions held by the Japanese and the Nationalists by the end of October 1938 were to remain largely unaltered until 1944. After fierce resistance to the Japanese in 1937–1938, Chiang adopted a largely defensive strategy. Some industries and universities were moved west to Chongqing but most industries were taken over by the Japanese. Inflation became rampant during the war and the Nationalist administration became increasingly corrupt.

: By October 1938, the Japanese had occupied a vast area of northern and eastern China and coastal areas in the south, occupied by 170 million Chinese. However, the Japanese lacked the manpower to takeover all of China.

Phase two (1939–1944)

The Sino-Japanese War trapped Japan into a long war of **attrition** whereas Japanese leaders had anticipated bringing Chiang Kai-shek quickly to accept a negotiated peace favourable to Japan. However, Chiang announced in December 1937 a *"sustained strategy of attrition"* and refused to negotiate with Japan (Tohmatsu and Willmott, p.57).

Attrition: strategy of wearing down an enemy in a long conflict

Frustrated by Chiang's refusal to negotiate, the Japanese turned to Wang Jingwei, a former Nationalist leader, and appointed him in March 1940 to head a puppet Chinese regime. Japanese forces used terror against the Chinese population in an attempt to end Chinese resistance, launching the 'Three-All Campaign': 'Kill All, Burn All, Loot All.' However, because of this Japanese brutality towards the Chinese, only a limited number of Chinese were prepared to collaborate with the invaders.

The Japanese attempted to advance southwards from the Yangzi but were held up by the GMD at Changsha in September 1939 and once more in September 1941 (Mawdsley, 2009, p.67).

In 1940 and 1941 the main Japanese focus was on two huge strategic bombing campaigns, aimed primarily at Chongqing. The Japanese expected to be able to break Chinese morale through these bombing raids but failed to do so.

Figure 1.11: **Chiang Kai-shek**

From December 1941 onwards, the Japanese had to devote most of their forces to their campaigns against the US and Britain in the Pacific but still had around 1 million troops in China. The war in China stalemated because the Japanese had insufficient resources to bring Chiang to surrender but neither the GMD nor the Chinese Communists (CCP) were able to seriously threaten Japanese control of the areas they had seized in 1937–1938. It is estimated that around 500,000 Japanese troops were killed fighting in China, whilst approximately 1,000,000 Chinese soldiers died (Mawdsley, p.68).

Phase three (1944–1945)

Operation Ichigo (April–December 1944): The Japanese launched a major offensive against the Chinese Nationalists in 1944, codenamed **Operation Ichigo**. This was directed against the Nationalists in south-central China and was aimed at destroying US bomber bases. In the process, they inflicted huge losses on the GMD, who suffered 500,000 casualties. In addition, 25% of the factories in areas under GMD control were destroyed.

Figure 1.12: **Japanese special naval landing forces in Shanghai**

The first half of 1945: The Japanese withdrew from southern China in order to concentrate on defending Manchuria. Soviet troops occupied Manchuria in August 1945, following the USSR's entry into the war against Japan less than a week before Japan surrendered.

1.3.1 RESPONSES: Political Developments within China—the Second United Front

By 1937 Chiang had decided that it was essential for the survival of his regime that he took a tougher line against Japanese incursions into China. Some of Chiang's own generals had kidnapped him the previous December at Xian for failing to try to combat Japanese aggression and forced him into agreeing to end the civil war with the CCP and conclude the Second United Front with the CCP, which he eventually did in August 1937.

Under the terms of the Second United Front, the Communists agreed to end their policy of 'sovietisation'—the confiscation and redistribution of landlords' land—and they also agreed that the Red Army, now renamed the **Eighth Route Army**, would operate under the command of Chiang Kai-shek. However, these promises were conditional on Chiang fulfilling his side of the agreement; he promised to abandon his attacks on the Communists, to allow other political parties to operate, and to establish a democratic system of government. However, the Second United Front did not work successfully.

Figure 1.13: **Chiang Kai-shek (Jiang Jieshi)**

Eighth Route Army: the new name for the 'Communists' army, previously called the 'Red Army'.

The Xian Incident of December 1936 and the prospect of a Second United Front between the GMD and CCP worried those Japanese who favoured further expansion into China as these developments threatened to present Japan with a more powerful, united enemy to deal with in China.

Chiang's response to the Marco Polo Bridge Incident (July 1937)

Despite the rising tide of nationalism in Japan, it appears that in July 1937 the Japanese authorities were not looking for full-scale war with China and that the initial skirmish between Japanese and Chinese troops just outside Beijing was not a premeditated act upon Japan's part in order to serve as a pretext for a full-scale invasion. It seems likely that Japan would have been content to resolve the dispute on the basis of Chiang Kai-shek making a few local concessions.

Chiang's response caught the Japanese by surprise as he decided to escalate the conflict, sending in Nationalist troops to reinforce those of the warlord who controlled the region and expanding the fighting to Shanghai. Chiang appears to have assumed that his stand would encourage either the US or the USSR to enter the conflict on his side. This proved to be a disastrous miscalculation by Chiang. By October 1937, Japan had sent 15 military divisions to the Chinese mainland.

Chinese Communist Party (CCP) campaigns against the Japanese

The war gave the CCP a great opportunity to expand their influence and control in northern China because, as the Japanese pushed south from Manchuria, they virtually ignored CCP forces, seeing the larger GMD armies as their main threat. This meant that much of northern China was left denuded of troops—both GMD and Japanese—and the CCP were therefore able to take control of much of the northern countryside by 1940. Then the CCP began attacking Japanese garrisons and lines of communication. This resulted in heavy casualties but the CCP retained control of much of this area.

Throughout the war, Mao's policy was to avoid set piece battles with superior Japanese forces and to engage instead in **guerrilla war**. The only large-scale offensive by the Red Army was the Hundred Regiments Offensive (1940), when General Peng Dehuai attacked the Japanese. The offensive failed and provoked terrible reprisals from the Japanese—this helped to foster a bitter hatred of the Japanese which the Communists were able to exploit.

Guerrilla war: method of warfare relying on ambushes and small-scale attacks on an enemy.

Mao's guerrilla campaigns had a political as well as a military purpose. By harassing the hated Japanese, the CCP achieved a heroic reputation among the Chinese peasants, who compared their efforts with the inactivity of the GMD armies. The Japanese estimated in 1945 that 75% of the engagements they had fought in China since 1937 were fought against the Communists. The war cost the Communists 100,000 casualties in the years 1941–1943 but enabled them to gain control of many rural areas in eastern China, which were behind enemy lines.

The Japanese, who by this time had more powerful enemies to contend with in the Pacific, left the Communists in charge of these rural base areas, and were willing to do so long as they did not harass their lines of communication. This gave the Communists the chance to win the hearts and minds of the peasants by implementing land reforms and introducing educational reforms and simple health care.

The international response to the Sino-Japanese War

The international response to the outbreak of the Sino-Japanese War proved very limited. This was largely because Britain and France's attention was increasingly focused on the threat posed by Nazi aggression in Europe, particularly from March 1938 onwards when Hitler invaded Austria. China did appeal to the League of Nations but Japan rejected a suggested international conference to meet in Brussels to try to end the war, a proposal that came out of discussions between the League and the US (Tohmatsu and Willmott, p.73). President Roosevelt made a speech in October 1937 in which he advocated the '**quarantine**' of aggressive states but no action followed on from his statement (Mawdsley, p.65).

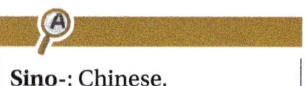

Sino-: Chinese.

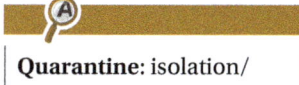

Quarantine: isolation/containment.

HISTORY SL & HL: THE MOVE TO GLOBAL WAR

Non-Aggression Pact: agreement in which participants promise not to attack each other

The Sino-Russian Non-Aggression Pact of August 1937

The USSR was the only country which offered any significant help to China in the period 1937–1941. Stalin wanted to ensure that Japan became bogged down in a long war in China and was therefore unable to attack the USSR.

The USSR sent China 1,300 warplanes and loans worth $250,000,000. 5,000 Soviet 'advisers' were sent to help Chiang Kai-shek, many of them serving as pilots (Mawdsley, p.65). However, once the USSR signed a non-aggression pact with Japan in April 1941, Soviet aid to China was reduced.

The ineffectiveness of the Second United Front

Though the Second United Front lasted until the end of the war in 1945, it proved to be a largely hollow agreement:

- There was no co-operation between the GMD and CCP in terms of resistance to the Japanese.
- Chiang broke his promise to establish a democratic system of government.
- Chiang made sure that very little of the aid which was sent to China by the USSR, and, later by the US and Britain, reached the Communists.
- For much of the war Chiang operated a blockade on the Communist Base Areas, a policy which was intended to prevent the spread of Communist influence but whose principal result was that it tied down tens of thousands of GMD troops who might have been fighting the Japanese. Chiang still regarded the Communists as his major enemy.
- In January 1941 GMD forces attacked the Communist New Fourth Army in Anhwei, near Nanjing. 10,000 Communists were killed but there were no further military clashes for the remainder of the war.

American aid to China (1941–1945)

When the US entered the Second World War in December 1941, President Roosevelt sent General Joseph Stilwell to China to coordinate US aid to Chiang. Stilwell and Chiang soon became very hostile to each other. Stilwell wanted Chiang to agree to wage war aggressively against the Japanese and to reform the GMD armed forces and administration, whilst Chiang wanted to retain his military equipment and use it sparingly, in order to be able to use it later against the CCP. He knew that the US would eventually defeat the Japanese regardless of what the GMD contributed in the war against Japan. However, Chiang's inaction seriously undermined the morale of the GMD army and lost the GMD the support of much of the Chinese population. It was only with great

Figure 1.14: **Chiang Kai-shek (Jiang Jieshi), his wife and General Stilwell in 1942**

reluctance that Chiang agreed to take part in expelling the Japanese from Burma. Roosevelt eventually replaced Stilwell with General Wedemeyer in an attempt to improve relations with Chiang.

In July 1944, a US Observer Group (known as the 'Dixie Mission') visited the CCP at Yanan and were impressed by their lack of corruption and vigorous campaigning against

1. CASE STUDY: JAPANESE EXPANSION IN EAST ASIA (1931–1941)

the Japanese. However, the US Government did not develop closer links with the CCP because it felt that it could not abandon their long-time ally, Chiang.

1.4 EVENTS: The Three Power/Tripartite Pact (1940); the Outbreak of War; Pearl Harbor (1941)

Japanese divisions over striking North or South

Historians nowadays largely reject the idea of Japan and the US being on an inexorable collision course from Japan's invasion of China in 1937 (or indeed earlier). However, as outlined below, there were longstanding tensions between the two countries and, in January 1940, Washington refused to enter into a new trade treaty with Japan on the expiry of the existing one.

Japanese decision-making was complex and inconsistent, indeed often hesitant, with a variety of factions looking to assert their preferred policy line. Certainly, until at least 1939, if not later, the Japanese armed forces were divided about the direction that Japanese expansion should take.

Military Faction	Strategy
North Strike Group	Seizing Siberia from the USSR: Japan and Russia had been rivals in Asia since the late 19th century, as both were keen to exploit the weakness of China. This rivalry had escalated to the point of war in 1904–1905, which resulted in a humiliating defeat for Russia. By the 1930s, Japan's leaders were extremely worried about the growth of Soviet power as Stalin embarked on a huge programme of rapid industrialisation.
South Strike Group	Attacking the colonies of Britain, France and Holland in South-East Asia: This was partly fuelled by resentment at what the Japanese perceived as unfair treatment at the hands of the US and the European colonial powers. They believed an attack on these colonies was possible without triggering war with the US.

Japanese-Soviet military clashes on the Manchurian/Mongolian border (1938–1939)

One factor that helped shape Japan's eventual decision to strike south was the defeat that Japanese forces suffered at the hands of the Red Army in May–September 1939 at Nomonhan on the Mongolian-Manchurian border, which resulted in approximately 18,000 Japanese casualties (Tohmatsu and Willmott, p.81). This followed on a smaller, but significant, clash around Changkufeng in July–August 1938. Japanese-Soviet disputes were eventually resolved in June 1940. However, it is clear that Japan continued to consider the option of an attack on the USSR, in spite of Japan's signature of the Non-Aggression Pact with the USSR in April 1941, right up to August 1941.

Source C: Louise Young points out the need to consider the long-term origins of Japan's attack on the US:

> Japan's tensions with the United States had deep roots. The two had begun to jockey for strategic domination of the Pacific before the turn of the century, when a rivalry over Hawaii precipitated a war scare and ended in the American decision to annex. The two powers fought over who should inherit the German-held Pacific islands after the First World War; they prepared war plans and built up their navies against one another. Tensions rose in the 1930s with Japanese aggression in China and a new naval arms race, but America did not take concrete action to stop Japan until it felt its position in the Philippines threatened by Japan's southward advance.(Young, p.168)

Practice question

For Question 1, part (a):

What, according to Source C, were the long-term causes of the war between Japan and America that broke out in 1941? [3 marks]

Japan announces a New Order in East Asia (July 1940)

Prince Konoe's cabinet drew up a policy document known as *The Main Principles of Basic National Policy* in which the Japanese government declared its intention to create a 'new order' in East Asia. At this stage, the Japanese government decided to strengthen its links with the Axis powers, work towards a non-aggression pact with the USSR, and, look to take over the European powers' Asian colonies.

Figure 1.15: **Prince Konoe**

With the surrender of France in June 1940, Nazi Germany's conquest of much of Western Europe and Britain facing the threat of Nazi invasion, Japan saw a golden opportunity to seize Dutch, British and French colonies in South-East Asia. Japan's military and political leaders affirmed that, if circumstances proved favourable, Japan should advance south, which would bring it into confrontation with Britain and the US. Mikiso Hane sees this as *"a crucial turning point in Japan's road to the war in the Pacific."* (Hane, 2001, p.311)

1. CASE STUDY: JAPANESE EXPANSION IN EAST ASIA (1931–1941)

The Tripartite Pact (September 1940)

In September 1940, Japan signed the Tripartite Pact with Germany and Italy. Germany, Japan and Italy agreed *"to assist one another with all political, economic and military means when one of the three Contracting Parties is attacked by a power at present not involved in the European war or in the Sino-Japanese conflict"* (Lamb and Tarling, 2001, p.172). The three signatories recognised each other's spheres of influence in Europe (Germany and Italy) and East Asia (Japan) and Germany renounced its claim to the former colonies it had owned in the Pacific prior to the First World War, which Japan had subsequently acquired. However, the pact included no binding military commitments. Hitler saw the pact as a means by which he could deter the US from intervening to help Britain. He told Mussolini that *"a close co-operation with Japan is the best way either to keep America entirely out of the picture or to render her entry into the war ineffective."* (Rothwell, 2001, p.186)

The signing of the pact followed a period of strained relations between Japan and Germany resulting from Japanese anger at Hitler's concluding the Non-Aggression Pact with Stalin in August 1939. Japan had felt betrayed by the conclusion of this pact and responded by withdrawing from the Anti-Comintern Pact.

The month before the conclusion of the Tripartite Pact, Japanese foreign minister, Yosuke Matsuoka, announced that Japan would look to create a **Great East Asian Co-Prosperity Sphere**.

Great East Asian Co-Prosperity Sphere: mutual economic support between the countries of East Asia

Japan's advance into northern Indo-China (September 1940)

The key moment in bringing about a hardening of American policy towards Japan was Japan's advance into Indo-China in 1940. Japan took the opportunity, provided by the defeat of France in June 1940, to induce the new **Vichy French** government to allow Japanese troops to occupy part of northern Indo-China in September of that year.

The Japanese-Soviet Non-Aggression Treaty (April 1941)

The signing of this non-aggression pact did not mean that, at this stage, the Japanese government had finally resolved on expanding south and given up on the possibility of an advance north at the expense of Soviet Russia.

Vichy French: the term by which the new French government became known after its surrender to Germany in June 1940. The new government was based in the town of Vichy because the Germans occupied Paris.

Japan takes the decision to expand to the south and occupies southern Indo-China (July 1941)

One factor that led Japan to decide to expand southwards was the capture by the Nazis of British cabinet documents in November 1940 when they intercepted the *Automedon*. The Nazis passed this intelligence onto Japan, which showed that the British government had concluded that it could not send a fleet to the Far East and could not defend Singapore against a Japanese attack (Tohmatsu and Willmott, p.90). This knowledge seems to have encouraged the Japanese to advance further into southern Indo-China in July 1941 and to step up plans for the seizure of European and American possessions in South-East Asia.

Japan's thrust into southern Indo-China posed a clear threat to Malaya, Singapore and the Dutch East Indies.

Japan's attack on Pearl Harbor (December 1941)

In the months after the American **embargo** of July 1941, Japan pursued two highly divergent policies: it tried to negotiate with Roosevelt's administration to end the American embargo, whilst at the same time preparing for a war with the US. The Japanese

Embargo: trade ban

Prime Minister, Prince Konoe, seems to have genuinely tried to pull the armed forces back from a military confrontation with the US, but, on 30 August, the Japanese army supported the Japanese navy's demand that war be commenced by the end of October.

On 25 September, Konoe's government decided on a postponement of war until the end of November, to allow more time to achieve a diplomatic breakthrough in negotiations with Washington. Konoe appears to have hoped that he could reach a compromise with the US whereby Washington would reopen trade with Japan in return for a partial Japanese withdrawal from China, but not from Manchuria or Korea. When this final attempt at diplomacy failed in mid-October, Konoe resigned, and, was replaced by the ultra-nationalist General Hideki Tojo.

Why did Japan attack Pearl Harbor on 7 December 1941?

Following the imposition of the American oil embargo, Japan was faced with two options:

1. a humiliating climb-down in the face of American pressure and the loss of the Chinese and Indo-Chinese resources that Japan had recently acquired; or,
2. going to war with the US and the European colonial powers in order to take control of the economic resources it needed, particularly the oil of the Dutch East Indies and the rubber of British-controlled Burma.

The Japanese realised that they could not defeat the US in a long war, given the US's economic strength. However, they calculated that, through a surprise attack on Pearl Harbor, they could eliminate the American Pacific fleet for a period of between nine months and a year and so have a free hand in the Pacific to acquire the resources they needed. Such an attack had first been seriously considered back in February 1941. The Japanese government assumed that this would be sufficient time for Japanese forces to dig themselves in so securely that the US would not have the stomach for a long war of attrition to evict them and would instead prefer to settle for a negotiated peace with Japan, allowing Japan to keep much of what it had conquered.

Figure 1.16: **Japanese naval aircraft prepare to take off from an aircraft carrier to attack Pearl Harbor during the morning of 7 December 1941**

Japan's leaders were acutely aware that, as American rearmament gathered pace, the disparity between Japanese and American forces would grow ever greater; they calculated that, in late 1941, Japan's naval strength was equivalent to 70% of the US's but that this would rapidly fall to a mere 30% by 1944.

1. CASE STUDY: JAPANESE EXPANSION IN EAST ASIA (1931–1941)

EXAM PRACTICE 4

Source D: General Tojo, Japanese Prime Minister, on 5 November, 1941, addressing the Japanese Imperial Conference:

> *The first stage of the war [with the US] will not be difficult. We have some uneasiness about a protracted war. But how can we let the United States continue to do as she pleases...? Two years from now we will have no petroleum for military use...When I think about the strengthening of American defences in the south-west Pacific, the expansion of the American fleet, the unfinished China Incident [war with China], and so on, I see no end to difficulties...I fear that we would become a third-class nation after two or three years if we just sat tight.*
>
> Cited in *From Versailles to Pearl Harbor*, Lamb and Tarling, p.176

Practice question

For Question 2:

With reference to its origins, purpose and content, analyse the value and limitations of Source D for a historian studying the origins of the Pacific War. [4 marks]

1.4.1 RESPONSES: International Response, including US Initiatives and Increasing Tensions between the US and Japan

The US had studiously avoided confrontation with Japan in the 1930s, refraining from intervention during the Manchurian Crisis in spite of Secretary of State Stimson's advocacy of **economic sanctions** against Japan. Even the full-scale Japanese invasion of China in 1937 did not lead to any departure from the US's policy of isolationism. Victor Rothwell points out that what triggered the start of a change in US policy was the series of Japanese announcements in 1938 about their desire to establish a 'New Order' in East Asia, culminating in Prime Minister Fumimaro Konoe's call, in November, for a union between Japan, Manchukuo and China (Rothwell, p.144). This alarmed the American government as it seemed to threaten US economic interests in the region.

Economic sanctions: restricting trade with a country as a form of political pressure

The American response to Japan's occupation of northern Indo-China (September 1940)

President Roosevelt responded to Japan's occupation of northern Indo-China by embargoing scrap metal and aviation fuel exports to Japan—a small step, but indicative of his determination to take a tougher line with Japan.

Back in July, Congress had passed the **Two-Ocean Naval Expansion Act** that provided for a massive programme of naval construction: 11 battleships, 27 cruisers, 115 destroyers and 43 submarines—evidence that the US was at last responding seriously to the Japanese threat (Tohmatsu and Willmott, p.83).

Japan could not match this programme, despite increasing its military expenditure massively, which, by late 1939, amounted to 65% of its total spending.

US-Japanese relations deteriorated sharply in 1941 as the US gradually, from January onwards, increased economic sanctions on Japan, banning trade in almost every raw material and metal.

Japan found it increasingly difficult to withstand the pressure of economic sanctions because its attempt to achieve economic self-sufficiency through the **Miyazaki Plan (August 1936)** failed. The plan was intended to prepare the Japanese economy to support total war and included provision for the production of synthetic oil; however, by 1941, synthetic oil production had only reached 8% of the planned target (Tohmatsu and Willmott, p.85). Even adding in domestic crude oil production, Japan was only producing 15% of its oil requirements by 1941. Likewise, Japan was highly dependent on imports for many other raw materials, including 71% of its iron ore and 20% of its rice and wheat consumption (Tohmatsu and Willmott, p.88).

The US's reaction to Japan's occupation of southern Indo-China (July 1941)

The key moment in the deterioration of Japanese-American relations came in July 1941 when the US government embargoed all fuel exports to Japan. The embargo was in reaction to Japan's occupation of southern Indo-China in July 1941 and was also applied by Great Britain and the Netherlands.

It appears that Roosevelt had been planning something short of a total ban but that lower level officials proceeded to announce a complete embargo and that proved popular with the US public. Japan might still have pulled back from the brink of war but US demands were tough, including the evacuation by Japan of all Chinese territory they had occupied since 1937. Only on that basis would the US lift the fuel embargo. Japan only had stockpiles of oil to last for two years.

Figure 1.17: **Roosevelt signing the declaration of war on Japan**

One reason for the failure of the US and Japan to resolve their differences diplomatically was that Roosevelt and his advisers were very largely preoccupied with developments in the European war, particularly after the German invasion of the USSR in June 1941. Another factor was that Roosevelt seems to have assumed that the Japanese, conscious of the US's far greater economic resources, would avoid fighting a war they could not win.

As Tohmatsu and Willmott observe:

> *"The American leadership assumed that the Japanese high command would appreciate the inevitability of defeat in a war with the United States and, in the final analysis, hold back. From this basic misreading of the Japanese national leadership flowed the errors that beset American policy in the second half of 1941."*
>
> (Tohmatsu and Willmott, p.85)

1. CASE STUDY: JAPANESE EXPANSION IN EAST ASIA (1931–1941)

1.5 Suggested Points for Practice Questions on Japanese Expansion

On Source A on page 6:

For Question 1, part (b):

What is the message conveyed by Source A? [2 marks]

- China is being carved up by the European Great Powers, and they are competing with each other in taking Chinese territory; they are eyeing each other up suspiciously.
- Japan is pensively watching the European powers carving China up.

On Source B on page 16:

For Question 1, part (a):

Why according to Source B did the League of Nations fail to stop Japan's takeover of Manchuria? [3 marks]

- Britain, France and the US did not yet see Japan as such a great threat to their interests in the Far East to lead them to take action against Japan.
- France regarded Japan as a potential ally in the fight to stop the spread of communism and disorder in Asia.
- Britain, France and the US were distracted by their domestic economic problems, which they put as a higher priority than addressing Japanese aggression.

On Source C on page 26:

For Question 1, part (a):

What according to Source C were the long-term causes of the war between Japan and America that broke out in 1941? [3 marks]

- American-Japanese rivalry for domination of the Pacific dating back to the late 19th century
- American-Japanese rivalry over the former German colonies in the Pacific following Germany's defeat in the First World War
- a naval arms race between Japan and the US, which resumed in the 1930s.

On Source D on page 29:

For Question 2:

With reference to its origins, purpose and content, analyse the value and limitations of Source D for a historian studying the origins of the Pacific War. [4 marks]

- ▶ **Origins**: It comes from General Tojo, the Japanese Prime Minister, a month before the attack on Pearl Harbor. **Value**: It is a private speech to senior Japanese officials and is therefore likely to be candid. It also provides insight into Japanese motives and assumptions immediately prior to the start of the Pacific War. **Limitations**: It provides only one Japanese perspective, not that of other Japanese leaders, and only a Japanese viewpoint, not that of other countries, notably the US.

- **Purpose**: Its purpose was to persuade the Japanese leadership of the necessity to launch the attack on Pearl Harbor. **Value**: It explains Japanese militarists' concern not to bow to US pressure and lose influence in Asia. **Limitation**: It may understate Tojo's concerns about taking on the US in order to maintain support for the war

- **Content**: It outlines Japanese motives for going to war and the leadership's calculations that the war was likely to be easy in the short-term but less so in the longer-term. **Limitation**: It does not indicate all of the reasons for the Pacific War, e.g. American hostility towards Japan's occupation of Indo-China.

1.6 A Complete Set of Practice Source-based Questions: The Manchurian Crisis

Source A: David Low, a cartoonist, depicts Japan's reaction to the League of Nations' Lytton Report in a cartoon entitled 'Trial by Geneva', published in the *Evening Standard*, London (November 1932).

> The full report can be found here: <https://filestore.nationalarchives.gov.uk/pdfs/small/cab-24-235-CP-404-1.pdf>. (Accessed 12 October 2021)

Figure 1.18: **'Trial by Geneva'**

Judge: The Court orders you to respect the law and sentences you to a good talking to.

Al Japan: And I order the Court to mind its own business and I sentence it to go and chase itself.

1. CASE STUDY: JAPANESE EXPANSION IN EAST ASIA (1931–1941)

Source B: Extract from the Lytton Report (1932), produced by Lord Lytton, the chairman of the commission of investigation set up by the League to look in to the Manchurian Crisis.

There is probably nowhere in the world an exact parallel to this situation [in Manchuria], no example of a country enjoying in the territory of a neighbouring State such extensive economic and administrative privileges. A situation of this kind can possibly be maintained without leading to incessant complications and disputes if it were the sign and embodiment of a well-considered and close collaboration in the economic and the political sphere. But in the absence of these conditions, it could only lead to friction and conflict.

Source C: John Costello, a British author and broadcaster, writing in an academic book, *The Pacific War* (London: Collins, 1981).

The League responded by sending a commission of inquiry led by Lord Lytton to investigate the situation in Manchuria. The Japanese made little attempt to hide the consolidation of their control of what was now a mainland **satellite** state even while the League Commission under Lord Lytton was in Manchuria on its fact-finding investigation…The Lytton Commission's report in January 1933 was far from the total condemnation that Washington expected. However, the League's refusal to recognise Manchukuo was enough to precipitate Japan's withdrawal as her Kwantung Army marched southwest toward Peking into Jehol Province, and the militarists in Tokyo believed they had now shed themselves of all restraint.

Satellite: a country under the control or influence of another

America's consistent refusal to invoke [bring into play] nothing more than words in support of the League and the treaty system her own diplomats had engineered had shown just how toothless and helpless the international community was when it came to upholding and enforcing the fragile framework on which peace rested. A dangerous precedent had been set.

Source D: Richard Overy, a British professor of history, writing in an academic book, *The Road to War* (London, 1989, p.54).

The Manchurian Incident caused a profound reappraisal of Japan's position within the international system. Until 1931, she had been regarded as a loyal but junior member of the concert of nations. From 1931 onwards two distinct interpretations of Japan's international status began to develop. For some Westerners, the issue was clear-cut: Japan had used force in Manchuria, so she became a pariah-state, the first government to defy the League of Nations: the only plausible Western response was ostracism [exclusion] or some form of punishment. The strongest advocates of a hard line were the Far East specialists in the [American] State Department, although their policy proposals often fell on deaf ears in Washington. There were many more supporters for a soft line: the military and naval adventurism was, they whispered, only temporary. If Japan could be seen to 'benefit' from the international system, then the Militarist cause would wither…Britain and the United States had huge investments in both China and Japan; 300,000 jobs in the United States depended on the Japanese silk trade…The Western governments did not want to invite retaliation by precipitate action over Manchuria…

1.6.1 Questions

1. (a) What, according to Source D, are the reasons why the League of Nations took a soft line against Japanese aggression during the Manchurian Crisis? [3 marks]

HISTORY SL & HL: THE MOVE TO GLOBAL WAR

(b) What is the message conveyed by Source A? [2 marks]

2. With reference to its origins, purpose and content, analyse the value and limitations of Source B for a historian studying the Manchurian Crisis. [4 marks]

3. Compare and contrast what Sources C and D reveal about the responses of the League of Nations and the US to the Manchurian Crisis. [6 marks]

4. Using the sources and your own knowledge, analyse the reasons why the League of Nations failed to stop Japan's aggression in Manchuria. [9 marks]

1.6.2 Some Suggested Responses

1. (a) According to Source D, the League took a weak line against Japan during the Manchurian Crisis partly because Western governments were divided in their responses to Japanese aggression between those who advocated a hard line and those who favoured a soft line. D also argues that Western governments took a soft approach because they were worried that taking tougher action might jeopardise their valuable trade with Japan. Thirdly, D suggests that Western governments shied away from confronting Japan because they feared that this might provoke Japan in to attacking them.

   (b) The message of Source A is that the League of Nations' decision to use moral condemnation as punishment was ineffective with regards to Japan since it was able to invade Manchuria without any repercussions. We can see the man representing Japan mocking the League and undermining its authority. The only response that the League appears to make is to puzzle over the 'Lytton Report' and not stop Japan. Japan's disregard for the League is emphasised in the caption, where Al Japan *"orders the Court to mind its own business"* and *"chase itself."* Similarly, the League is made to seem ineffectual as it only *"sentences"* Japan *"to a good talking to."*

2. Source B's origin is that it is an extract from the Lytton Report, commissioned by the League of Nations, and is valuable to a historian as it outlines Lytton's findings from the investigation, undertaken during the Manchurian crisis, into the Mukden Incident and, in particular, examines the circumstances that led to Japan's takeover of Manchuria. The content is valuable because it suggests that, as a consequence of Japan's extensive concessions in Manchuria, a confrontation between China and Japan was always likely and this, perhaps, partly explains why the League decided not to take stronger action against Japan. It is also useful because its purpose is to show what the League of Nations' formal and public response to the Manchurian Crisis was, prior to the Assembly voting on the Lytton Report. However, one limitation is that it only indicates part of Lytton's report in to the Manchurian Crisis, relating to why the crisis occurred and does not refer to the report's recommendations nor how either the League or Japan responded to the report.

3. Both sources mention the lack of support that America gave the League in dealing with Japan's invasion of Manchuria. Source C refers to America's *"consistent refusal"* to use nothing more than words to uphold international law. Similarly, Source D explains how, because so many American jobs depended on the silk trade with Japan, the US did not want to confront Japan over its occupation of Manchuria. Both sources also suggest that the League took a weak line in the face of Japanese aggression, with

1. CASE STUDY: JAPANESE EXPANSION IN EAST ASIA (1931–1941)

C referring to the toothless and helpless response of the international community, whilst D makes it clear that advocates of *"a soft line"* far outnumbered those in favour of taking stronger action against Japan and, therefore, a strong line was not taken.

On the other hand, the sources differ in several ways. Firstly, Source C, whilst examining the League's weak response, places more blame on America than does Source D, which refers to both *"Britain and the United States"* as having interests in Japan that prevented them from taking action, and refers to the *"Western Governments."* A second difference is that, while Source C suggests that the impact of the US and League's weakness was momentous, as *"a dangerous precedent had been set"*, Source D does not, in fact, make an explicit point about the longer-term impact of the League and America's lack of action. Furthermore, whilst D suggests that there were differences of response within the international community, saying that *"two distinct interpretations of Japan's international status began to develop"*, C's analysis implies that the League was united in the line it took. Finally, whereas C analyses the US's response in general terms, D differentiates between hard- and soft-liners at Washington who differed over how best to respond to Japan's aggression.

4. Source C suggests that the *"international community"* was *"toothless and helpless"* in addressing Japanese aggression. One of the reasons why the League failed to stop Japanese aggression was that the League had no ready recourse to military force. The League had no standing army of its own, had not developed agreed protocols for raising peacekeeping forces, and was reliant on support from its member countries as a result. Given that there was no requirement to provide military forces, and that the League's strongest members were suffering from the effects of the Great Depression, there was very little chance that these countries would have agreed to provide troops to enforce the League's authority in the face of Japanese aggression. Furthermore, the League's ability to take military action depended on the willingness of Britain and France to act as world policemen and neither had sufficient forces in East Asia to have forced Japan to withdraw from Manchuria. Source D refers to the concerns of western governments, particularly the US and Britain, that they would lose out economically if their trade with Japan was severed as a result of their taking a strong line against Japan; D points out that 300,000 American jobs depended on the silk trade with Japan.

The slow response of the League was also a factor in the failure to stop Japan's aggression in Manchuria. This was partly a result of China initially using Article 11 of the Covenant to appeal to the League, which allowed Japan to block the appeal, and also because of the slow progress of the Lytton Commission whose report was not published until October 1932, over a year after the Mukden Incident. The League's slow response undoubtedly was also a product of divided opinions within the League over how to deal with Japan's aggression, which Overy outlines in Source D.

It is also clear that one reason why the League of Nations did not take strong action against Japan was that some governments did not view Japan as solely to blame for the Manchurian Crisis. For example, as it says in Source C, *"the Lytton Commission's report… was far from the total condemnation that Washington expected."* As suggested in Source D, some western diplomats believed that, if a soft line was adopted towards Japan, Japan might see that it could *"benefit from the international system"* and that militarism in Japan would weaken. This line was a plausible one to take since, up until the Mukden Incident, Japan had co-operated with the international community since the First World War, signing up to the Washington Naval Treaties and playing a key role in the League itself as a permanent member of the Council. Furthermore, Source B, in suggesting that Japan's unique position in Manchuria made confrontation between Japan and China very likely, implies that members of the League may have viewed the Manchurian Crisis as partly China's fault, rather than just Japan's. In particular, because Chiang Kai-shek had just come to power in China in 1927 and was committed to ending foreign concessions, some western governments may have seen Chiang as a threat to their interests and sympathised with Japan's occupation of Manchuria as a pre-emptive step to prevent Chiang from obliging Japan to give up its concessions in that region. Sympathy for Japan's position would have been strengthened by the fact that Manchuria had been a lawless region under warlord control rather than strongly under the control of the National government of China and its predecessors. A further consideration for western governments in wishing to avoid confrontation with Japan was that many in the West saw Japan as a useful bulwark against Soviet expansion in the Far East.

Another reason why western governments and the League found it more difficult to deal with Japan's takeover of Manchuria is because of the complex political situation in Japan. The Mukden Incident was orchestrated by Japan's Kwantung Army, stationed in Manchuria, and was not initiated by the Japanese government. In May 1932, Japan's Prime Minister, Inukai, was assassinated by nationalist elements within the armed forces because he was trying to restrain their aggression. The growing influence of the militarists in Japan, referred to by Source D, made it much more difficult for the League to negotiate effectively with Japan.

As Source C suggests, one of the principal causes of the League's failure was the absence of support from America, and its *"consistent refusal to invoke nothing more than words."* America's refusal to join the League almost a decade earlier had already been the cause of much controversy, and it is likely that its lack of support may have been what primarily kept the League from being taken seriously by other nations. However, Source D does point out that American officials were divided in their response to the Manchurian Crisis and that some favoured taking a hard line against Japan. This was certainly the case with Henry Stimson, the US Secretary for State, who favoured imposing sanctions; but, as D indicates, in the end advocates of a softer approach, including President Hoover, prevailed. Without American support, the League almost certainly would have felt that economic sanctions would prove ineffective. What the sources do not refer to is that the absence of the USSR from the League also weakened the latter's response as only the USSR and the US had significant military forces in the region.

In conclusion, although some of the sources might suggest that the reasons the League failed were because the League did not view Japan's actions as wrong, or because the members of the League were only looking out for their own countries' interests, the main reason that the League failed was because it lacked the ability to apply either effective economic or military sanctions. The League only scolded Japan, sentencing it to *"a good talking to"*, as portrayed by Source A, because it could not do anything more forceful.

Chapter 2: Case Study: German and Italian Expansion (1933–1940)

2.1 Causes of Expansion

2.1.1 The Impact of Fascism on Italy's Foreign Policy

Historians are divided over:

- the extent to which Mussolini's foreign policy was shaped by **fascist ideology**.
- how far Mussolini's foreign policy marked a break with that of the liberal era that preceded his rule.

	'Anti-fascist' historians (De Felice, Gentile)	'Fascist/ideological' historians (Blinkhorn, Knox)
What drove Mussolini's foreign policy?	**Pragmatism/geopolitics:** • Italy's geographical position, history, and circumstances in the 1920s and 30s drove foreign policy. • Mussolini's more expansive foreign policy in the 1930s was simply a response to changing international circumstances. The impact of the Great Depression and Hitler's rise to power created new opportunities for Italian expansion as the leading democracies (Britain, France and the US) prioritised economic recovery and Hitler's increasingly aggressive foreign policy disrupted the international order established by the Paris peace settlement of 1919–1920.	**Ideology:** • Italy's aggression of the late 1930s and early 1940s was the logical outcome of the fascist belief in struggle and violence. Mussolini saw an aggressive foreign policy as essential in order to transform the Italian people into a dynamic, aggressive and united nation. • Mussolini had long-term foreign policy objectives, shaped by fascist ideology. • In the 1930s Mussolini was at last able to discard the cautious approach of the 1920s in order to realise those aims.

Fascist ideology: authoritarian and ultra-nationalist ideas promoted by a number of right-wing movements in Europe in the 1920s and 1930s.

Pragmatism: decision-making shaped by practical concerns.

Geopolitics: the influence of geographical factors on a country's policies.

HISTORY SL & HL: THE MOVE TO GLOBAL WAR

	'Anti-fascist' historians (De Felice, Gentile)	**'Fascist/ideological' historians** (Blinkhorn, Knox)
Why did Mussolini eventually ally with Nazi Germany?	**Pragmastism:** • Mussolini was looking to expand Italy's territory and influence, but not committed to any predetermined programme. • Mussolini might have decided to ally with democratic Britain and France rather than Nazi Germany if he had believed such an alliance would serve Italy's interests best. In the end, Mussolini believed that his best opportunity for expansion would be provided by an alliance with Hitler.	**Ideology:** • The German alliance and Italy's aggression of the late 1930s and early 1940s were the logical outcome of the fascist belief in struggle and violence and of the shared ideological outlook of Fascist Italy and Nazi Germany. • MacGregor Knox (1982) stresses the interdependence of fascist foreign and domestic policy, "internal consolidation was a prerequisite of foreign conquest and foreign conquest was the decisive prerequisite for a revolution at home." Knox sees violent struggle, whether at home or abroad, at the heart of fascism.

Mussolini's foreign policies in the 1920s—some continuity with the past

- During the 1920s, Mussolini's foreign policy had much in common with that of the **liberal governments** before and after the First World War, as he aimed to expand Italy's influence in the Balkans, Near East and East Africa.

- In the 1920s Mussolini largely appeared prepared to play by the rules of western diplomacy, and Italy had an important role in the League of Nations. Mussolini was for the most part content to co-operate with Britain and France, the strongest European powers in the 1920s who dominated the areas Mussolini was keen to expand in, namely the Mediterranean and North Africa.

The explanation for the relatively peaceful and restrained policy conducted by Mussolini during the 1920s lies in the fact that much of his attention was focused on extending and then consolidating his political position within Italy. Furthermore, much of the Italian army was tied up in suppressing rebellion in Libya.

- However, Mussolini's methods were certainly different from those of his liberal predecessors. He was hasty and reckless, prone to make grandiose gestures and, above all, keen to increase Italian prestige and his own. As Philip Morgan suggests,

> "It was not so much that Mussolini was 'moderate' in the 1920s, as that his ambitions were effectively checked by British and French control of European affairs, an international situation which Italy was not powerful enough to change on her own."
>
> Philip Morgan (1998), p.63

Liberal governments: governments committed to maintaining Italy's parliamentary system and individual liberties

Even in the 1920s, Mussolini demonstrated a preference for confrontation and aggression:

▶ **The Corfu Crisis (1923)**

Mussolini sent troops to occupy Corfu, after the murder of an Italian general allegedly by Greek bandits, in an attempt to bully Greece into paying compensation

2. CASE STUDY: GERMAN AND ITALIAN EXPANSION (1933–1940)

to Italy. It is possible that Mussolini had planned to take over Corfu permanently, but he withdrew after the League of Nations ordered Greece to pay Italy compensation.

▶ **Mussolini sought to undermine France, Italy's main traditional rival for influence in the Mediterranean and North Africa:**

- He encouraged opposition movements in France's Moroccan and Tunisian colonies.
- He was hostile to Yugoslavia, an ally of France, because it had gained territory Italy had wanted at the end of the First World War. Mussolini funded Croat separatists who sought independence from Yugoslavia.

▶ **Albania (1926)**

Mussolini helped Ahmet Zog seize power in Albania (1926) and turned Albania into a **client state**, to extend Italy's influence to the south of Yugoslavia. Zog proclaimed himself King Zog I in 1928.

Figure 2.1: **King Zog of Albania**

Client state: a country dominated by another state

Mussolini's foreign policy in the 1930s: increasingly expansionist and pro-German

Mussolini's foreign policy from the mid-1930s became increasingly aggressive. Some historians explain this development as a response to the growing economic difficulties that Italy faced as a consequence of the Great Depression and to the changing international situation, which provided opportunities for Italian expansion as Britain and France were preoccupied by their own economic problems and by German and Japanese expansionism.

Other historians, such as Blinkhorn, argue that Mussolini's motivation was ideological and that, after a relatively cautious approach in his first decade in power, in the 1930s his regime became more radical as he sought to achieve long held aims for 'living space', similar to those of Hitler. Furthermore, Blinkhorn (1984) argues that Mussolini believed that he needed to go to war to keep fascism alive, that Mussolini was anxious, and, by the early 1930s, that *"his movement and regime were growing too comfortable, too paunchy and middle-aged and needed new challenges."*

Source E: Mussolini's announcement of Italy's declaration of war in June 1940:

Figure 2.2: Benito Mussolini

We want to break the territorial and military chains that are strangling us in our own sea. A nation of 45 million souls is not truly free unless it has free access to the ocean...This gigantic struggle is only one phase of the logical development of our revolution...it is the struggle of young and fertile peoples against sterile ones who stand on the verge of decline; it is the struggle between two centuries and two ideas.

Quoted from Delzell (1971), p.214

Practice question

For Question 2:

With reference to its origins, purpose and content, analyse the value and limitations of Source E for a historian studying Mussolini's foreign policy. [4 marks]

2.1.2 The Impact of Nazism on Germany's Foreign Policy

The impact of the First World War and the Versailles Treaty on German foreign policy

The **Paris Peace Treaties** helped create a strong nationalist movement in Germany intent on destroying Versailles. The new democratic government of Germany was obliged by the Allies to accept peace terms at Versailles in June 1919. Unfortunately for the **Weimar Republic**, many nationalists blamed the new Socialist government for agreeing to the **Armistice** in November 1918 and for signing the Versailles Treaty, claiming that the German army could have fought on, if it had not been stabbed in the back by cowardly, democratic politicians.

Many historians conclude that the Versailles Treaty constituted a dangerous half-way house between generous and harsh treatment of Germany. Germany was punished enough for many Germans to want revenge but insufficiently to be made impotent; by the mid-1930s Germany, in spite of its loss of territory and raw materials at Versailles, had recovered its strength to become once more the dominant industrial and military power in Europe.

Even in the 1920s, before Hitler's rise to power, many, if not most, German politicians were committed to recovering the lands lost to Poland in the east. Although it is true that during the mid-1920s Gustav Stresemann, the German foreign minister, pursued a policy of 'fulfilment' of co-operation between Germany and its former enemies, Britain and France, Stresemann was not prepared to enter into guarantees over Germany's eastern frontiers. By contrast, Stresemann did, as part of the **Locarno Pact (1925)**, recognise

---

Paris Peace Treaties: the treaties drawn up in Paris and imposed on the defeated countries by the victor countries at the end of the First World War.

Weimar Republic: the new German republic, which came into being after the Kaiser's abdication. It was known as such because its founding constitution was drafted in the town of Weimar.

Armistice: the ceasefire that ended the fighting in the First World War.

Locarno Pact (1925): the agreement signed at the Locarno Conference held in Switzerland by which France, Belgium and Germany agreed to recognise their mutual borders.

2. CASE STUDY: GERMAN AND ITALIAN EXPANSION (1933–1940)

Germany's borders in the west, as laid down by Versailles. Nonetheless, Stresemann's success in negotiating agreements with regards to **reparations**, German entry into the League of Nations, and early Allied withdrawal from the Rhineland showed that Germany could win revisions of the Treaty of Versailles by negotiation rather than having to resort to force.

Reparations: financial penalties imposed on Germany by the Treaty of Versailles

How central was ideology to Hitler's foreign policy?

Foreign policy was of primary importance to Hitler, whose main priority from 1934, once he had established his dictatorship, was to rearm Germany, ready for expansion.

Hitler's foreign policy was largely shaped by his radical theories about race, and was only partly a reaction to the Treaty of Versailles. Although there is no doubt that Hitler aimed to reverse many of Versailles' key terms, it is much too simplistic to assert that the Versailles Treaty made the rise of Hitler and a second world war inevitable.

Figure 2.3: **Hitler (1933)**

What were Hitler's foreign policy aims?

There is a major historiographical debate about Hitler's aims, part of which is summarised below:

	'Intentionalist' historians (e.g. Dahrendorf)	'Functionalist'/'structuralist' historians (e.g. Craig)
What drove Hitler's foreign policy?	**Ideology:** Hitler viewed the Aryan race as the master race, and he also believed in **Social Darwinism.**	**Geopolitics:** Germany's geographical position, history, and circumstances in the 1930s drove foreign policy.
What did Hitler want?	Hitler wanted to establish an empire in Eastern Europe up to the Ural Mountains, colonised by the Aryan race, with the Slavs becoming a slave race; this marked a fundamental break with traditional, nationalist German policy.	Hitler was like earlier German politicians, including Wilhelm II and Stresemann: Hitler wanted to make Germany the dominant power in central/eastern Europe by overturning Versailles.
How far did Hitler follow predetermined goals?	**Master planner:** He pursued consistent objectives that he put forward in *Mein Kampf* (1925) and the *Zweites Buch* (1928) ("Second Book"), and outlined in his speech, which was recorded in the Hossbach Memorandum (1937).	**Opportunist:** Hitler simply took advantage of opportunities to expand as they arose, with no fixed goals or plans.

Intentionalist: historian who argues that Hitler's policies were determined by his racial ideology and the goals he set; this perspective sees Hitler as driving events

Functionalist/structuralist: historian who argues that Hitler's policies were shaped by the circumstances in which Hitler found Germany in 1933, and by its history and geography; this perspective sees Hitler as driven by events

Social Darwinism: the belief that different races are involved in a struggle for survival/domination and that the strong will takeover the weak

The line that this guide broadly follows is that of the 'intentionalist school' that views Hitler as radically different from more traditionally-minded German nationalists. This view is supported by the fact that many of the conservative German diplomats and generals who had served under the Weimar Republic, and who were prepared to serve Hitler in the early to mid-1930s, were removed (particularly in 1938), after the scope of Hitler's plans for wars of conquest became apparent.

EXAM PRACTICE 6

Source F: Hitler writing in *Mein Kampf* (1925):

> *And so we **Nationalist Socialists** consciously draw a line beneath the foreign policy tendency of our pre-war period. We take up where we broke off six hundred years ago. We stop the endless German movement to the south and west, and turn our gaze towards the land in the east. At long last we break off the colonial and commercial policy of the pre-war period and shift to the soil policy of the future.*
>
> Adolf Hitler, pp.597–8

National Socialists: also known as Nazis.

Practice question

For Question 2:

With reference to its origins, purpose and content, analyse the value and limitations of Source F for a historian studying Hitler's foreign policy. [4 marks]

Breaking the restrictions that Versailles had imposed on Germany's armed forces was a prerequisite for expansion. Hitler's racist ideas meant that he was committed to the creation of a **Greater German Reich**, incorporating all German-speakers. Revising the Versailles Treaty was, for Hitler, not the ultimate goal but a means towards the larger aim of winning *Lebensraum* (living space).

Hitler sought *Lebensraum* for the German '**master race**' and also the acquisition of *Grosswirtschaftsraum* (greater economic space), areas which had the resources that Germany needed. Hitler envisaged a Germany that would include the whole of Eastern Europe and the western part of the USSR. The native peoples of the area, mainly Slavs and regarded by the Nazis as '*untermenschen*' (sub-human), would work for the Germans as slaves.

Greater German Reich: The concept of a German empire.

Master race: Nazi view of the German 'Aryan' people as superior to all others.

2.1.3 The Impact of Domestic Economic Issues on the Foreign Policies of Italy and Germany

The impact of the Great Depression on Italy

Mussolini, during the 1920s, with the exception of his occupation of Corfu in 1923, followed a relatively peaceful and restrained policy because much of his attention was focused on domestic political consolidation and in subduing rebellion in Libya. However, the Wall Street Crash (1929) hit Italy hard, with unemployment rising to over 2 million by 1933. The government obliged industrial workers to accept wage cuts in 1930 and 1934, whilst agricultural wages dropped by between 20 to 40% during the 1930s.

The growing economic difficulties facing Italy appears to have been one of the factors that account for Mussolini's increasingly aggressive foreign policy in the 1930s. Mussolini's invasion of Abyssinia in 1935–1936, was, in part, an attempt to revive domestic support for his regime.

The Abyssinian invasion led to Italy's withdrawal from the League of Nations and to Mussolini reorienting his diplomatic ties. He broke his links with Britain and France and sought ever closer relations with Hitler's Germany, joining the Anti-Comintern Pact in 1937 and ultimately signing a military alliance with Germany—the so-called 'Pact of Steel'—in May 1939. Mussolini's support from 1936 onwards was one factor that gave Hitler the growing confidence to challenge Britain and France and revise the post-First World War territorial settlement in the East.

The impact of the Great Depression on Germany

In the case of Germany, its economic recovery in the mid-1920s was very fragile and highly dependent on the continuation of US loans. The Great Depression was the key factor in the collapse of the Weimar Republic and led to the rise of Hitler, with his attendant aggressive foreign policy in the period 1933–39. The year before the advent of the Great Depression, the Nazis polled under 3% of the votes in the 1928 Reichstag elections; in 1930, as unemployment soared in Germany, the Nazis gained 17% of the seats in the German parliament and became the second biggest party. With unemployment peaking at 6 million in 1932, the Nazis became the largest party in the Reichstag with 37% of the seats; President Hindenburg therefore decided to appoint Hitler chancellor in January 1933.

Within months Hitler had established a single party state and, by 1935, was sharply accelerating German rearmament. Under Hitler, Germany quickly revived as the most powerful industrial and military power in Europe; with an aggressive dictator in charge, driven by a racial vision of winning *Lebensraum* in the East for the 'master race', both the Paris peace settlement and the international order were to be challenged and disrupted from the mid-1930s onwards.

2.1.4 Changing Diplomatic Alignments in Europe

The 1930s saw major realignments in European diplomatic relations, which facilitated the aggressive policies of Hitler and Mussolini and undermined Britain and France's resolve in standing up to German and Italian aggression. These will be explored in greater detail later on but, at this stage, they can be summarised as follows:

1. **Italy moved from being suspicious of Hitler's Germany to a position of friendship and ultimately an alliance with Germany.**

    The period 1933–1935 saw Mussolini wary of Hitler's ambitions to expand, particularly into Austria, and led Italy to sign the **Stresa Front** with Britain and France in 1935. However, the Abyssinian Crisis (1935–1936) undermined Italy's relations with Britain and France and led Mussolini to sign the **Rome-Berlin**

Figure 2.4: **Mussolini and Hitler, at the time of the Axis agreement, October 1936**

Stresa Front: the agreement signed by Britain, France and Italy at the Italian resort of Stresa in 1935 in which they promised joint action against any country breaking the Versailles Treaty.

Rome-Berlin Axis: the friendship agreement signed by Mussolini and Hitler in 1936.

Axis in 1936. This diplomatic turnaround gave Hitler greater confidence in accelerating his plans for expansion.

2. **Poland's alliance with France was partially undermined by Poland's Non-Aggression Pact with Germany in 1934.**

   France's defence strategy placed a great importance on the alliances that it had signed in the 1920s with a number of East European states in order to contain Germany. Hitler's signing of the Non-Aggression Pact with Poland worried France as it suggested that it might not be able to count on Poland's support to prevent German expansion.

3. **Belgium renounced its military pact with France and moved to a position of neutrality in 1936.**

   French defence planning up until March 1936 was based on the assumption that it could count on Belgium as an ally to help defend France's border against a German attack; this dated from a French-Belgian military accord of 1920. However, in 1936 Belgium declared its neutrality, leaving the Franco-Belgian border as a potential gateway for a German invasion of France.

4. **Stalin moved from isolation in the early 1930s to a position of seeking, in the mid-1930s, to forge links with France and Britain in order to contain Nazi Germany.**

   As part of this strategy, the USSR joined the League of Nations in 1934 and signed treaties with France and Czechoslovakia in 1935. Stalin also provided military aid to the **Republicans** in the Spanish Civil War (1936–1939). However, Stalin was increasingly frustrated by the lack of progress in achieving meaningful security agreements with the western democracies and so ultimately turned instead to an accommodation with Hitler.

5. **The Nazi-Soviet Pact (August 1939)**

   Securing the non-aggression pact with the USSR encouraged Hitler to believe (wrongly) that France and Britain would take no action when he invaded Poland on 1 September 1939.

Republicans: forces fighting in support of Spain's democratic government.

Non-Aggression Pact: the Nazi-Soviet Pact of 1939 under which Germany and the USSR agreed not to go to war against each other.

2.1.5 The End of Collective Security

Collective security: maintaining peace and the mutual security of countries through joint action against aggressor states.

Why did collective security break down in the 1930s?

1. The most important single factor in undermining collective security in the 1930s was *the impact of the Wall Street Crash* (October 1929) and *the ensuing Great Depression*.

   The Great Depression dislocated the international economic system and created huge unemployment and social distress. In the US, by 1933, 25% of the labour force was unemployed; in Germany, the official figure for unemployment in 1932 was 6 million.

   One consequence of this was that the Great Depression undermined confidence both in the capitalist system and in parliamentary democracy. The effects of the Great Depression were felt around the world but two of the most badly hit economies were those of Germany and Japan, and these two countries went on to pose the greatest threats to the international order.

2. CASE STUDY: GERMAN AND ITALIAN EXPANSION (1933–1940)

The crash on the New York Stock Exchange on Wall Street started on 29 October 1929; 16 million shares were sold at much reduced prices. Share prices continued to fall until July 1933, by which time they were at a level of only 15% of their value in October 1929. The Wall Street Crash was only one cause of the Great Depression alongside wider causes such as the financial instability of many European countries and the fall in world agricultural prices. The Great Depression was different from the periodic recessions that occur in the world business cycle, in that it lasted much longer and economic output fell much more sharply. In 1931–1933, a banking crisis hit the US and many parts of Europe as thousands of banks collapsed.

Many governments reacted to the Great Depression by trying to protect their own industries from foreign competition by means of raising **tariff** barriers against imported goods. In 1930, the Hawley-Smoot Tariff, passed by Congress, greatly restricted foreign imports but, in the process, sparked off a tariff 'war' with other countries, for example, in 1932 Britain and its imperial partners set up the Imperial Preference System which discriminated in favour of members of the Empire but discriminated against goods from outside the Empire. World trade fell by about two-thirds in the period 1929–1932 and even by 1938 it was still only 40% of what it had been in 1929.

Tariff: a tax on imported goods.

EXAM PRACTICE 7

Source G: The British historian Richard Overy, in *The Inter-War Crisis* (p.80), outlines the impact of the Great Depression on international relations:

> The economic crisis…did more than anything else to sour relations between the major states and to bring to an end the era of internationalist collaboration. Policies of economic selfishness revived old grievances and created new ones. Resentments that had simmered beneath the surface in the 1920s burst into the open with a fresh urgency. The social consequences of the slump [Great Depression] pushed populations in the weaker economies towards political extremism and violent national self-assertion.

Practice Question

For Question 1, part (a):

What according to Source G was the impact of the Great Depression on international relations? [3 marks]

---

2. The *League of Nations was undermined* by the Japanese invasion of Manchuria (1931) and Germany's and Japan's withdrawal from League membership (1933).
3. *Hitler came to power* in Germany (1933), intent on revising the Versailles Treaty.
4. The Great Depression *deepened the US's commitment to isolationism*, reducing the likelihood of US intervention to uphold peace through collective security.

The US had withdrawn into isolationism in the 1920s following the Senate's failure to ratify the Treaty of Versailles. The US consequently never joined the League of Nations and Woodrow Wilson was succeeded by a trio of Republican presidents who remained wary of entangling the US in diplomatic or military agreements.

The effect of the Great Depression was to lead US politicians to withdraw even further from international collaboration and to put US economic interests before all else. In July 1933, President Roosevelt blocked agreement at the World Economic Conference in London, by refusing to take joint action to stabilise currency exchange rates.

In 1935, the US Senate passed a provisional Neutrality Act, and this was followed in 1937 by a full Neutrality Act, which committed the US government to neutrality in the event of future wars between foreign countries. The US's reluctance to involve itself in international crises in the 1930s in part explains the weak stance taken by Britain and France in dealing with acts of aggression by Germany, Italy and Japan.

2.1.6 Appeasement

Britain's policy of making concessions to Hitler in the hope that this would make Hitler behave more reasonably and thus maintain peace in Europe is known as appeasement.

As Andrew Crozier puts it:

> *"It became the basic principle of British foreign policy from the end of 1935 onwards to seek a European and general settlement that would in effect replace the peace settlement of 1919 and bring all the European states into satisfactory treaty relations with one another. This is what was meant by appeasement: the **pacification** of Europe through discussion and negotiation. Germany was, of course, the focus of such a policy…"*
>
> Crozier (1997), p.94

Pacification: bringing about peace.

Figure 2.5: **Neville Chamberlain (centre), on his visit to Hitler at Berchtesgaden in September 1938**

What factors shaped Britain's policy of appeasement?

1. From the late 1920s Britain began to pursue a policy of making some revisions to the Versailles Treaty in Germany's favour, for example, withdrawing the Allied army of occupation from the Rhineland five years ahead of schedule. This stemmed from the conviction that some of Versailles's restrictions on Germany had been unreasonably

harsh. From Hitler's accession to power in 1933 until March 1939, when Hitler occupied non-German speaking parts of Czechoslovakia, the British government believed that the most effective way of preserving European peace was to continue a policy of negotiating limited changes to the Versailles Treaty.

The Great Depression, as seen above, had given rise to Hitler's regime in Germany and made the foreign policies of Japan and Italy more aggressive; hence, Britain was faced with the prospect of a variety of challenges to its interests and to the international order. Appeasement was Britain's response: thereby the British government hoped to avoid a war with either Hitler or Mussolini whilst the Japanese appeared to pose a growing menace to British interests and possessions in the Far East. Britain and France were very conscious of how vulnerable to Japanese attack their colonies in Asia were and of the threat that a Japanese attack might encourage revolt by nationalist movements within their empires.

2. The British government was preoccupied with resolving the economic problems caused by the Wall Street Crash. This was one reason why it delayed rearmament until 1934.

3. The British government was reluctant (as was France) to confront Germany because they could not count on support from the US, which was following an isolationist foreign policy during the 1930s. The US had been isolationist in the 1920s but the Great Depression strengthened this attitude.

4. British politicians were concerned about the possibility of being dragged into a European conflict at a time that there was growing unrest in several parts of its Empire, for example in India and in its League of Nation's **Mandate** of Palestine.

5. Equally important in accounting for appeasement was the strong current of pacifism evident in Britain in the 1930s; in 1935, a Peace Pledge Union was organised which staged a ballot in which 9 million people voted to reject war. This mood was echoed in France when crowds numbering a million demonstrated in May 1936 in favour of peace. Memories of the horrific slaughter of the First World War meant that many people, both in Britain and France, were committed to the prevention of another war.

6. The desire to avoid another war was reinforced by knowledge of the effects of bombing of civilians during the Spanish Civil War (1936–1939).

Mandate: a former colony of the Ottoman (Turkish) Empire entrusted by the League of Nations to Britain to administer while preparing for its independence.

France's position

Just as with Britain, the Great Depression's impact on France made its leaders much less inclined to stand up to Hitler's violations of the Versailles Treaty in the 1930s. French preoccupation with bringing down unemployment and reviving economic output—French steel production, even in 1938, was still one-third below what it had been in 1928—took priority over rearmament; France only started rearming seriously in 1936. From 1928, France had spent huge sums on constructing a massive series of fortifications on its border with Germany, known as the **Maginot Line**.

Maginot Line: fortifications named after Andre Maginot, the French Minister of War.

Figure 2.6: **Edouard Daladier (French Prime Minister), leaving the Munich Conference, September 1938**

The French government felt too weak to prevent Hitler breaking the Versailles Treaty unless Britain took joint action alongside France. British politicians, on the other hand, were more favourably disposed towards German revisions of the treaty as long as this was done through negotiation. So in practice, in spite of the threat posed to French security by Hitler's rearmament and other treaty violations, France did very little to prevent Hitler breaking the Versailles Treaty until it declared war on Hitler in September 1939.

France's serious political divisions also explain its passive attitude towards Hitler's aggression; many on the Right in France were more concerned about their own Communist Party and the threat of Soviet expansion than Hitler.

2.2 *EVENTS:* **German Challenges to the Post-war Settlements (1933–1938)**

Germany's withdrawal from the Disarmament Conference and the League of Nations (1933)

Hitler detested the League of Nations and was just looking for a pretext to extricate Germany from multi-lateral disarmament talks, so that he was free to embark on rapid rearmament. The League's Disarmament Conference had initially convened in Geneva in 1932 and had already seen France and Germany clash: the German government had insisted on parity with France; either France (whose army numbered 600,000) should disarm down to Germany's level (100,000) or Germany should be allowed to rearm up to France's.

When the Geneva Disarmament Conference reconvened, Ramsay MacDonald, the British Prime Minister, outlined a scheme whereby France, Germany, Italy and Poland would gradually move, over the course of 5 years, towards approximate parity in terms of numbers of troops. In an attempt to reassure the French, MacDonald also proposed that Germany would not have full access to all categories of weapons and that French forces stationed in parts of the French Empire would be in addition to the level fixed for the European armies, so that France's total armed forces would still be greater than Germany's. However, MacDonald's proposals met with stiff criticism from France and more restrained objections from Germany. The Conference again adjourned in May 1933.

When the Disarmament Conference reconvened in October 1933, Hitler withdrew from the Disarmament Conference, using France's refusal to allow German parity as an excuse, and also gave notice that Germany would leave the League of Nations. The disarmament

2. CASE STUDY: GERMAN AND ITALIAN EXPANSION (1933–1940)

conference was effectively killed off by the German walk-out, although, having adjourned in October 1933, it briefly reconvened for a final, fruitless session in May 1934.

The impasse over the balance of armed forces between France and Germany had given Hitler exactly what he had been hoping for—the freedom to rearm more openly, which he proceeded to do. There had been limited, secret German rearmament under the Weimar Republic but Hitler increased the scale of this in 1933–1934, although it was not until March 1935, that Hitler publicly repudiated the military restrictions laid down at Versailles.

Why was Hitler initially cautious in challenging the post-war settlements?

In 1933–1934 Germany's armed forces were considerably weaker than those of its neighbours such as France and Poland. Germany's army numbered little more than 100,000, whilst France's was 600,000 strong.

German-Polish Non-Aggression Treaty (January 1934)

Before seriously starting on rearmament, Hitler signed a 10-year friendship treaty with Poland in January 1934, thus reassuring the Poles. Hitler certainly remained committed to winning back Germany's lost lands from Poland but it is possible that he saw in Poland a potential client-state that might act as an ally against the USSR. In 1934 Hitler told Rauschnigg, a leading Nazi in **Danzig**, that *"All our agreements with Poland have a purely temporary significance. I have no intention of maintaining a serious friendship with Poland."* (Overy, p.54)

Danzig: A city taken from Germany by the Treaty of Versailles which gave it the status of a 'free city'.

Undoubtedly Hitler saw the Non-Aggression Pact as a way to undermine France's security system in eastern Europe; France had signed alliances with Poland and Czechoslovakia in the 1920s in order to contain Germany.

Austrian Nazi *Putsch* (July 1934)

It is possible that Hitler was behind the Austrian Nazis' attempt in July 1934 to seize power in Vienna in order to achieve the *Anschluss* (union with Germany), which had been forbidden by both the Treaty of Versailles and the **Treaty of St. Germain**. Hitler certainly openly supported the Austrian Nazis in the period leading up to their attempted coup but seems to have believed that they could seize power without direct aid from Germany.

Putsch: A German word, used to mean an attempt to seize power by force.
Anschluss: union of Germany and Austria.

In their abortive coup on 25 July, the Austrian Nazis murdered the Austrian Chancellor, Dollfuss, who had very close ties to Mussolini. The **putsch** failed and Kurt Schuschnigg, an opponent of the Nazis, became chancellor. The incident alarmed Mussolini so much that he mobilised 10,000 Italian troops at the Brenner Pass on the Austro-Italian border. Most contemporaries believed that Hitler was behind the attempted Austrian Nazi *putsch* but historians, on the whole, doubt that was the case.

Hitler's challenges to the post-war settlements (1935–1936)

1. **Reunion with the Saar (January 1935)**

In January, over 90% of the inhabitants of the Saar, administered by the League of Nations since 1920, voted in favour of reunion with Germany. This was in accordance with the Treaty of Versailles and the **plebiscite** was supervised by the League of Nations. This

Plebiscite: a referendum or vote.

strengthened Germany's economy, as the Saar was rich in coal, and boosted Hitler's popularity within Germany.

2. **The reintroduction of conscription and Hitler's announcement of rearmament (March 1935)**

In March 1935 Hitler announced that, contrary to the Treaty of Versailles, he was reintroducing military conscription and that he intended to create an army of 550,000 men. He also revealed that German already had begun to build an air force in breach of Versailles. These announcements alarmed Britain, France and Italy, who consequently came together in the short-lived Stresa Front (April 1935), under which they pledged co-operation against further breaches of the Paris peace treaties.

Although Mussolini was a fascist, he was concerned about Hitler's declared aim of achieving the *Anschluss*. This was because Italy had gained the South Tyrol, a German-speaking area, in the Treaty of St. Germain and Mussolini feared that if Hitler took over Austria, he would then demand the South Tyrol. Furthermore, if Germany took over Austria, Mussolini suspected that Hitler might look to expand into the **Balkans** where Mussolini had his own ambitions.

Balkans: a region in South-Eastern Europe.

3. **The Anglo-German Naval Convention (June 1935)**

Britain angered France and Italy by signing the Anglo-German Naval Agreement in June 1935, allowing Germany to have a navy with a tonnage 35% that of Britain's. This meant that Britain had, just nine weeks after signing the Stresa Front, **unilaterally** sanctioned a breach of the military restrictions laid down by the Treaty of Versailles, because a German navy 35% the size of Britain's would far exceed the limitations imposed on Germany in 1919.

Unilaterally: acting on its own, without the agreement of other countries.

4. **Re-militarising the Rhineland (March 1936)**

Hitler generally proved adept at reading how his opponents were likely to respond. Encouraged by the collapse of the Stresa Front, because of the Anglo-German Naval Convention and the Abyssinian Crisis, and by the international community's preoccupation with the Abyssinian Crisis, he felt confident enough to remilitarize the Rhineland, a breach of both the Versailles Treaty and the Locarno Pact (1925). Although the League of Nations condemned this action, France and Britain did nothing about it. Hitler's generals were astonished; they had advised against the move, believing it would provoke a military confrontation with the much larger French Army.

Diplomatic realignments

In 1936–1937 Hitler worked to strengthen Germany's diplomatic position:

1935–1936:	During the Abyssinian Crisis, Germany continued to trade with Italy in spite of the League of Nations' sanctions on Italy, which damaged Italy's relations with Britain and France.
July 1936:	Hitler and Mussolini both sent troops and planes to fight alongside the forces of the rebel Nationalist General, Francisco Franco, in the Spanish Civil War.

Figure 2.7: **German bomber, part of the Condor Legion sent to Spain**

2. CASE STUDY: GERMAN AND ITALIAN EXPANSION (1933–1940)

October 1936: Hitler and Mussolini signed the Rome-Berlin Axis, a friendship treaty.

November 1936: Germany and Japan signed the Anti-**Comintern** Pact, an agreement to co-operate to prevent the spread of Communism.

Comintern: the agency set up by Lenin to promote worldwide revolution.

Ideology as the driver for Hitler's Foreign Policy: The Hossbach Memorandum (November 1937)

Many historians see the **Hossbach Memorandum**, the record of a meeting Hitler held on 5 November 1937 with key military and diplomatic personnel, as evidence that Hitler's foreign policy objectives were much more radical than that of traditionally-minded German nationalists. However, there are others, notably A. J. P. Taylor, who question its significance. Taylor argues that, in this speech, Hitler was merely *"daydreaming"* and that it did not represent a clear indication of Hitler's intentions (A. J. P. Taylor, p.48).

Memorandum: a note or record.

In the speech Hitler outlined his plans for *Lebensraum*, which he said needed to be achieved by 1943–1945, because, by then, other countries would have completed their rearmament. Hitler spoke about the need to achieve *Anschluss* with Austria and to destroy Czechoslovakia:

> *"The aim of German policy was to make secure and to preserve the racial community and to enlarge it. It was therefore a question of space.*
> *The German community comprised over 85 million people and, by reason of their number and the narrow limits of habitable space in Europe, it constituted a tightly packed racial core such as was not to be found in any other country and such as implied the right to a greater living space than in the case of other peoples."*
>
> From the 'Hossbach Memorandum', cited in Lee, p.106

Five weeks after the **Hossbach Conference**, **Plan Green** was adopted by the German armed forces: this laid down a plan for the invasion of Czechoslovakia (Rothwell, p.77).

Some of Hitler's generals and diplomatic officials, who were non-Nazis, expressed their concerns at his expansionist plans and the danger of provoking a general European war. Over the next few months, Hitler removed these doubters, including Constantin von Neurath, the Foreign Minister, Werner von Fritsch, the Commander-in-Chief of the Army, and Werner von Blomberg, the War Minister. In addition, 18 generals were obliged to retire. Joachim von Ribbentrop replaced Neurath as Foreign Minister. Furthermore, Hitler abolished the War Ministry and replaced it with the OKW (*Oberkommando der Wehrmacht*: Supreme Command of the Armed Forces), assuming personal command of the armed forces.

Oberkommando der Wehrmacht: Supreme Command of the Armed Forces.

Hitler had now very largely cut his links with the military and diplomatic personnel he had inherited from the Weimar Republic. In the same vein, Hitler had replaced Schacht as his economics minister in November 1937 because Schacht opposed the pace of rearmament and the strains this was imposing on Germany's economy.

From 1936 onwards, the pace of Hitler's foreign policy accelerated sharply, disrupting international relations in the process. Up until 1937, Hitler had been hoping to reach an understanding with Britain but, from 1937 onwards, he regarded Britain as an obstacle to his expansionist plans.

Further German challenges to the post-war settlements: Austria and Czechoslovakia (1938)

1. **Achieving the *Anschluss* (March 1938)**

   At the beginning of 1938, Hitler had no plans for an immediate takeover of Austria, seemingly intent on gradually increasing Germany's influence over Austria, and yet, in March, the *Anschluss* was achieved. This demonstrates that while Hitler had certain consistent aims, he was an opportunist when it came to timing and methods. By 1938, Hitler was seeking to bring closer the union of Germany and Austria, with a view to eventually absorbing Austria into the German Reich.

   In February 1938, Hitler invited Austria's Chancellor, Kurt Schuschnigg, to a meeting at Berchtesgaden, where Schuschnigg was bullied into making concessions, including the appointment of the leading Austrian Nazi, Artur Seyss-Inquart, as Interior Minister and an agreement that Austria would co-ordinate its economic and foreign policies with those of Germany. However, once he returned to Vienna, Schuschnigg tried to regain the initiative by announcing, on 9 March, that a plebiscite would be held in which the Austrian people would be given the chance to vote on whether they wanted Austria to remain *"a free and German, independent, Christian and united"* country (Royal Institute of International Affairs, 1944). Hitler, fearing that an unsupervised plebiscite might go against him, used the threat of force to compel President Miklas to sack Schuschnigg in favour of Seyss-Inquart, who immediately invited the German army into Austria.

   Figure 2.8: **Hitler with Artur Seyss-Inquart, the Austrian Nazi leader**

   Following an unopposed invasion on 12 March, the *Anschluss* was proclaimed. In a Nazi-supervised plebiscite, 99% of those who voted expressed their approval of the *Anschluss*. Neither Britain nor France had the will to resist Hitler, partly because most Austrians appeared to support the *Anschluss*.

2. **The Sudeten Crisis (September 1938)**

   It appears that Hitler sought to pick a quarrel with the Czech government over the **Sudetenland** in order to provide an excuse for destroying Czechoslovakia.

Sudetenland: the mainly German-speaking region of Czechoslovakia.

Why did Hitler seek the destruction of Czechoslovakia?

1. He saw the Czechs as an inferior race and had resented them since his time growing up within the old Austro-Hungarian Empire.

2. Czechoslovakia had been created by the hated 1919–1920 Peace Settlement and included over 3 million Sudeten Germans who had, in Hitler's eyes, been denied the

2. CASE STUDY: GERMAN AND ITALIAN EXPANSION (1933–1940)

right of self-determination (they had formerly been part of the old Austro-Hungarian Empire).
3. Czechoslovakia was a democratic state.
4. Czechoslovakia was an ally of both France and the USSR and had an efficient army; it constituted an obstacle to Hitler's plans for expansion eastwards.

The *Anschluss* left Czechoslovakia, Hitler's next target, in a vulnerable position, with German troops along its southern as well as its northern border. In seeking to gain control of Czechoslovakia and its strong armaments industry, Hitler carefully built up links with the Sudeten German Party led by Konrad Henlein.

March 1938:	Hitler instructed Henlein to keep on raising his demands in order to prevent an agreement between the Czech government and the Sudeten Germans. As Richard Overy puts it, the Sudeten Germans were used as *"a Trojan horse to achieve Hitler's aim of 'smashing' Czechoslovakia."* (Overy, p.47)
24 April:	In a speech at Karlsbad, Konrad Henlein demanded **autonomy** for the Sudeten Germans.
20 May:	The Czech government responded to false reports of German troop movements on Czechoslovakia's border by ordering mobilisation. France warned Germany that it would intervene if Czechoslovakia were attacked. Hitler was enraged by this mobilisation scare as it appeared that he had backed down in the face of Czech and French threats. On 28 May, Hitler told his ministers and generals that he would seek to destroy Czechoslovakia at the earliest opportunity; however, at this point, no date was fixed for a German invasion. Throughout the summer tension increased between the Sudeten Germans and the Czechs, in part stirred up by Nazi propaganda about alleged Czech persecution of the Sudeten Germans.
12 September:	At Nuremberg, Hitler made a furious speech in which he seemed to threaten the imminent invasion of Czechoslovakia. At this point, it appears that Hitler, intent on a short, victorious war against Czechoslovakia, was planning to invade, using the issue of the Sudeten Germans as his pretext, and confident that no country would come to Czechoslovakia's aid. However, Prime Minister Neville Chamberlain's subsequent diplomatic intervention caused Hitler to prevaricate and eventually agree to the transfer of the Sudetenland to Germany, putting on hold, for the moment, the destruction of the Czech state.
15 September:	Chamberlain visited Hitler at Berchtesgaden, and, during the next week, he and French Prime Minister Daladier devised a plan under which Czechoslovakia would be made to hand over to Germany any territory where more than 50% of the inhabitants were German. The Czechs had little choice but to agree since France was their main ally.
22 September:	Chamberlain met Hitler again at Bad Godesberg but Hitler increased his demands by asking for immediate occupation of the Sudetenland. War seemed imminent as the Czechs and their French allies began to mobilise and Britain also began to mobilise its navy. The Poles and the Hungarians, encouraged by Hitler, began to demand that parts of Czechoslovakia should be handed over to them.
	Chamberlain, in a last bid to preserve the peace, appealed to Mussolini to persuade Hitler to attend a conference to resolve the crisis. Hitler was advised against invading Czechoslovakia by leading Nazis, notably Göring, and was shaken by the lack of enthusiasm for war shown by the public at a military parade in Berlin on 27 September. Richard Overy argues that: *"There is no doubt that Hitler did not want a major war in 1938…He hoped to achieve a local victory over the Czechs and counted on Western weakness. Presented with the open risk of war in the West, he went against his instincts and gave way"* and agreed to meet with Chamberlain, Daladier and Mussolini at Munich on 29 September. (Overy, p.49)

Autonomy: self-government.

| 29–30 September: | The Czechs were not consulted and their ally, the USSR, was not invited. At the **Munich Conference**, the four powers agreed, on 30 September, that Germany should occupy the Sudetenland between 1–10 October. In addition, they agreed that, once Poland and Hungary's claims to Teschen and Ruthenia respectively were settled, the four powers would guarantee what was left of Czechoslovakia. Since France, the USSR, and Britain were not prepared to support the Czechs and they could not win a single-handed war against Germany, Benes, the Czech President, felt that he had no choice but to accept the terms of the Munich Agreement. Benes subsequently resigned on 4 October. |

Figure 2.9: **Chamberlain, Daladier, Hitler and Mussolini at Munich**

Non-committal: not involving a commitment to any course of action.

In return Hitler signed a **non-committal** document expressing a desire for a lasting Anglo-German peace. For the Czechs, the loss of the Sudetenland was a disaster, which deprived them not only of much of their vital industrial base, including 70% of their iron and steel resources, but also all of their strongest frontier defences. Shortly after Germany occupied the Sudetenland, Hitler remarked to Albert von Speer, *"What a marvellous starting position we have now. We are over the mountains and already in the valleys of Bohemia."* (Overy, p.49)

2.2.1 RESPONSES: International Response to German Aggression (1933–1938)

1. British, French and Soviet rearmament

Although Britain and France had failed to rearm prior to the mid-1930s, growing anxiety about the threats posed by Germany, Italy and Japan, led them to join in what became an international arms race similar to that seen in Europe before the First World War.

Soviet rearmament started in earnest under Stalin in 1930 and, by 1936, the USSR had built nearly 16,000 planes and just under 19,000 tanks; rearmament accelerated even more rapidly from 1937 onwards under Stalin's Third **Five-Year Plan**.

Britain began serious rearmament in 1934, with a programme of military spending amounting to £1,500 million in the period up to 1938.

France followed suit in 1936. Hitler accelerated his rearmament of Germany sharply in 1936, with his **Four Year Plan**, designed to make Germany ready for war by 1940.

Richard Overy calculates that, in total, military expenditure rose more than six-fold in the period 1934–1939 in Germany, Britain and Japan; in the USSR, eight-fold; and, in France, ten-fold.

Five-Year Plan: Stalin introduced a series of Five-Year Plans, starting in 1928, which laid down targets for rapid industrialisation of the USSR.

Four-Year Plan: in 1936 Hitler ordered his officials to draw up a plan for increasing raw material production in order to provide for rapid rearmament and make the German economy ready to support Germany's armed forces in a war by 1940.

2. Stalin's search for security in the 1930s

Faced by growing threats to the USSR, at a time when it was still far behind the West in terms of industrialisation, Stalin sought to increase Soviet security by ending the USSR's diplomatic isolation. For much of the 1930s, Stalin looked to the West for 'collective security' against the threat posed by Hitler but, eventually in 1939, Stalin did a complete about-turn and signed the Nazi-Soviet Pact.

- In 1934, the USSR was admitted to the League of Nations, with a permanent seat on the League's Council.
- In 1935, the USSR signed pacts with France and Czechoslovakia, committing itself to defend the latter against attack. However, the French government never ratified this agreement.
- At the Seventh Congress of the Communist International, Stalin's new strategy of organising an Anti-Fascist Popular Front was announced. The Popular Front encouraged an alliance of Communists and other left-wing parties throughout Europe to fight against fascism.

Figure 2.10: **Stalin with Voroshilov**

- Stalin sent aid to the Republicans in the Spanish Civil War (1936–1939). Stalin was concerned by German and Italian intervention on General Franco's side, so, from October 1936, the USSR provided the Republicans with tanks and planes and military advisers. Franco's Nationalists won in 1939.

Up until 1938, Stalin was looking to play off the western democracies against Germany. In the period up to May 1939, Maxim Litinov was the Soviet Commissar for Foreign Affairs who favoured closer links with the West.

3. Great Britain's response

In response to German expansion, Britain in the 1930s pursued a dual policy of simultaneously:

- seeking to maintain peace in Europe through negotiating an international settlement that revised the Versailles Treaty in order to satisfy German grievances.
- strengthening British security through rearmament.

British rearmament started slowly in 1934 and would not render Britain secure in the short or mid-term; in 1935 British military spending increased by 20% compared to 1934 and, by 1936, it had risen by 66% from the 1934 level. In 1938 it was four times higher than in 1934 and amounted to 38% of total government spending.

Throughout this period (1934–1939), the British government sought to ensure that rearmament levels did not impose too great a strain on the economy as ministers envisaged any war as likely to be a war of attrition in which economic strength would play a key part. The priorities of British defence spending were the Navy and increasing air defences with modern aircraft to guard Britain against bomber attacks. British ministers realised that rearmament would not be completed until 1939/40 at the earliest (Overy, *The Road to War*, p.75). This made the avoidance of war vital and strengthened the British government's efforts to pacify Hitler by means of concessions.

Appeasement

Arguably British foreign policy in the 1930s did not mark a fundamental change from that of the 1920s in the sense that, since the 1920s, British politicians had accepted that the Versailles Treaty was flawed and needed revising in order to maintain international peace.

Source H: Andrew Crozier writing about British foreign policy in the inter-war period in *The Causes of the Second World War* (p.90):

> For many years it was accepted that appeasement was a policy associated with the government of Neville Chamberlain who became Prime Minister in May 1937...[however] appeasement was not a phenomenon peculiar to Neville Chamberlain or the 1930s. It would indeed be misleading to imply that there was any change in the fundamental aim of British foreign policy...from the moment the Treaty of Versailles was signed, British policy was revisionist. What happened after 1930 was that the British government increasingly envisaged the necessity of revision on an hitherto unprecedented scale, deemed that an active role on its part was essential to this process and perceived that the time for enacting these revisions was short.

Practice question

For Question 1, part (a):

How far, according to Source H, did British foreign policy change in the 1930s? [3 marks]

At the Geneva Disarmament Conference in 1932–1933, the British representatives showed considerable sympathy towards German claims, arguing that the Versailles Treaty had been too harsh and that revisions should be made; they saw it as unreasonable that Germany should still be obliged, a decade and a half after the First World War had ended, to limit its armed forces as severely as Versailles laid down. The British government was critical of France's inflexible approach and blamed France for the failure to reach an agreement with Germany at Geneva.

The Stresa Front (April 1935)

Demilitarised zone: the area in which Germany could not station troops or build fortifications

Britain joined with France and Italy in condemning Hitler's announcement about rearming Germany far beyond the limits laid down by the Versailles Treaty and reintroducing conscription. The Stresa signatories also declared their determination to uphold the Locarno Pact, including the **demilitarised zone** in the Rhineland, and affirmed their commitment to Austrian independence and to oppose any further unilateral breaches of international treaties. However, the Stresa signatories did not agree on what action they might take in the event of Hitler breaking Versailles, and, in no sense was it a military alliance (Ross, 1983, p.88). Furthermore, Britain almost immediately undermined the Stresa Front by concluding the Anglo-German Naval Convention.

The Anglo-German Naval Convention (June 1935)

Britain did not consult either Italy or France before signing the Anglo-German Naval Agreement with Hitler in June 1935, which permitted Germany to expand its navy beyond the level laid down at Versailles, up to 35% of the size of the British navy. Britain was drawn into this naval agreement largely because of its fears that, with its navy already over-stretched, the Japanese were about to abandon the Washington Naval Treaty and London Naval Treaty limitations and embark on a major naval arms race. The British government was, therefore, keen to reach an agreement with Hitler in order to limit the growth of the

German navy rather than find itself involved in a new naval race with both Germany and Japan.

Figure 2.11: **The launching of the German battleship, Tirpitz**

Britain, in signing the naval convention, announced that it hoped that this would lead to a general treaty on arms limitations, but the agreement put a huge strain on Britain's relations with both France and Italy because Britain had condoned German violation of the Versailles Treaty without involving any wider international discussion and approval.

The Remilitarisation of the Rhineland (March 1936)

Britain condemned Hitler's sending of troops into the Rhineland and hosted a meeting of the League of Nations Council in London, which declared Hitler's action a breach of the Versailles Treaty. However, neither Britain nor the League, preoccupied with the Abyssinian Crisis, went beyond verbal condemnation. Privately there was some sympathy within the British government for the remilitarisation, given that the Rhineland had remained German territory and it was now 18 years since the end of the First World War. Lord Lothian remarked that the Germans had simply walked into their own backyard.

Chamberlain as Prime Minister (May 1937)

When Chamberlain became Prime Minister in May 1937, he sought a general settlement of European tensions, with disarmament, Germany's return to the League and a non-aggression pact, signed by western European countries to replace the Locarno Pact. He envisaged that making economic and colonial concessions to Germany would *"result in her being quieter and less interested in political adventures."* (Overy, p.84)

In November 1937, Chamberlain sent Lord Halifax to Germany to discover what changes Hitler was seeking and Halifax indicated to Hitler that Britain was not opposed to revisions of the Versailles settlement provided they were accomplished peacefully and by negotiation. Chamberlain followed this up in March 1938 by proposing colonial concessions to Germany, consisting of the transfer to Germany of either Portuguese or Belgian colonies in Africa. However, the German government abruptly rejected them.

The *Anschluss* (March 1938)

The British government had been expecting Germany to move towards increasing its control over Austria as the British Foreign Secretary, Anthony Eden, had told Joachim von Ribbentrop, the German ambassador to Britain, in December 1937. Although Britain protested at the German occupation of Austria and its annexation on 12–13 March, there was no prospect of Britain taking any action. It was widely believed in Britain that forbidding the union of Germany and Austria had been a key error of the Versailles settlement (Bell, p 264).

The Sudeten Crisis (March–September 1938)

Britain, having previously been largely detached from eastern European affairs, took a lead role in 1938 in trying to prevent the growing confrontation, on the one hand, between the Sudeten Germans and the Czech government, and, on the other hand, between Germany and Czechoslovakia, escalating to the point of war. Chamberlain was intent on resolving the Sudeten Crisis peacefully. He was very conscious of the lack of readiness for war of Britain's armed forces in 1938, and he also believed that both the Sudeten Germans and Germany had justifiable grievances against the Czech government. Konrad Henlein, the leader of the Sudeten Germans, had been warmly received on his visits to London in 1935 and 1937. Furthermore, Lord Halifax had indicated to Hitler privately in November 1937 that Czechoslovakia was one area of the 1919 settlement where there was scope for revision. Later that month, Chamberlain told representatives of the French government that the Sudeten Germans had legitimate grievances that needed redressing.

From the end of March 1938, the British government put pressure on its Czech counterpart to make concessions to the Sudeten Germans. However, Chamberlain also warned Germany that, if war broke out between Germany and Czechoslovakia, Britain might feel obliged to intervene (Bell, p 272). As P. M. H. Bell points out, Chamberlain was also intent on keeping the USSR out of any involvement in the Sudeten Crisis, in spite of the USSR's treaties with both France and Czechoslovakia. This stemmed from Chamberlain's intense distrust of communist Russia and his conviction that to involve the Soviets would render impossible any diplomatic solution of the Sudeten Crisis given Hitler's fervent anti-Communism (Bell, p 273).

As tensions increased between the Sudeten Germans and the Czech government and after a war scare in May 1938 when the Czech government partially mobilised in response to a false report of German mobilisation, the British and French governments put growing pressure on the Czech government to accept Henlein's demands.

July 1938	The French privately told the Czechs that France would not fight over the Sudetenland.
August	The British persuaded the Czechs to accept Lord Runciman as a mediator between themselves and the Sudeten Germans (Bell, p.276).
12 September	Following Hitler's aggressively anti-Czech speech at Nuremberg, it appeared that a German invasion of Czechoslovakia was imminent.
	The prospect of a German invasion of Czechoslovakia triggered Neville Chamberlain's intervention; over the following two weeks, Chamberlain flew to Germany on three occasions, in order to try to avert war.
15 September	Following his meeting with Hitler at Berchtesgaden on 15 September, Chamberlain persuaded the British and French governments to approve the transfer of the Sudetenland, after the holding of a plebiscite, to Germany. Britain and France then pressurised the Czech government into accepting this by threatening to leave them to fight Germany alone if war broke out.

2. CASE STUDY: GERMAN AND ITALIAN EXPANSION (1933–1940)

22 September	On his return visit to see Hitler at Bad Godesberg on 22 September, Chamberlain was shocked to discover that Hitler was now increasing his demands to the occupation of the Sudetenland by 1 October and to include the satisfaction of Polish and Hungarian territorial demands on Czechoslovakia (which Hitler had encouraged). The British and French governments rejected Hitler's new demands and both made preparations for war, with France starting mobilisation on 26 September and Britain mobilising its navy two days later (Bell, p.276).
	It appeared as if Europe was on the brink of war with Hitler planning an invasion of Czechoslovakia by 1 October and Britain and France, having done an about turn, prepared to go to war in defence of Czechoslovakia. However, Chamberlain was still hoping to achieve a diplomatic solution, and he, along with Mussolini, suggested an international conference to discuss the Sudeten Crisis. Hitler was unsure whether Britain and France were bluffing or not, so he bowed to pressure from his own advisors, most notably Goering, and, from Mussolini, and reluctantly agreed to attend a conference at Munich on 29 September.
29 September	At the Munich Conference, attended by Britain, France, Germany and Italy (but not Czechoslovakia or the USSR), it was agreed that the Sudetenland should be handed over to Germany by 10 October, with plebiscites held in areas with significant mixtures of Germans and Czechs living there. The four powers agreed to guarantee the new borders of Czechoslovakia while Chamberlain and Hitler signed a joint declaration of their countries' intentions never to go to war with each other.

4. France's response

The French government's attitude towards Hitler's expansionism differed markedly from that of Britain. Containment of Germany, not its conciliation, was France's objective (Henig, p.16).

France's main focus in terms of defence was the construction of the Maginot Line on her border with Germany. This had commenced at the end of the 1920s. The French government's strategy in the event of war with Germany was to secure its border by means of the Maginot fortresses, whilst waiting for British and, hopefully, in the longer term, American, assistance in order to defeat Germany in a war of attrition.

France resisted British pressure on it to make significant concessions to Hitler and instead tried to build a mutual defence pact against Germany, which included France's eastern European allies, Poland and Czechoslovakia, along with Russia and Italy (Henig, p 17). Britain supported the idea of creating an eastern European version of the Locarno Pact of 1925 but opposed any notion of such an agreement that did not include Germany; otherwise, Britain argued, Germany would feel encircled and might be provoked into aggression.

France looked to a pact with the USSR and Italy to contain Hitler

France, led by Foreign Minister Louis Barthou, pressed ahead in 1934 with its objective of securing a pact with Russia and Italy in order to contain Germany. This endeavour was encouraged by the USSR's entry in to the League of Nations in 1934. Barthou was assassinated in October 1934 and replaced by Pierre Laval, who visited Mussolini in Rome in January 1935. Laval and Mussolini agreed on the need to safeguard Austria's independence and Laval indicated that France would not oppose the extension of Italian influence in Abyssinia.

Figure 2.12: **Louis Barthou visiting Marshal Pilsudski in Warsaw, 1934**

The Stresa Front (April 1935)

Following Hitler's announcement that he was reintroducing conscription and building a peacetime army of 550,000 in defiance of the Versailles Treaty, France looked to achieve closer ties with Italy and Britain in an attempt to contain Germany. However, the Stresa 'Front' is a misnomer as it suggests a genuine, concerted commitment to joint action against any further German violation of either the Versailles or Locarno Treaties, whereas there was no substance behind the agreement reached at Stresa. Relations between Italy, on the one hand, and Britain and France, on the other, worsened markedly as a result of Mussolini's invasion of Abyssinia in October 1935.

The Franco-Soviet and Czech-Soviet Treaties of May 1935

Although France and the USSR signed a mutual assistance pact in May 1935, French politicians were deeply divided over the agreement, which was bitterly denounced by those on the right of French politics and was not approved by the French Chamber (Parliament) until February 1936. Even Pierre Laval who signed the pact was sceptical about it and mistrusted the Soviets. Laval seems to have seen it as a way of putting pressure on Germany with the ultimate goal of then negotiating an agreement between France and Germany. Laval refused to agree to French-Soviet military staff talks, which might have given the pact real substance. The French-Soviet pact was, in fact, extremely limited as it provided for mutual military assistance only in the event that an act of unprovoked aggression against either country was submitted to the League for its arbitration and verified by the signatories of the Locarno Pact.

The French-Soviet Pact was accompanied by a Czech-Soviet Treaty signed in the same month; this committed the USSR to defend Czechoslovakia if it were attacked, but only on the condition that France took action in defence of Czechoslovakia too.

France's strategy of seeking an Italian alliance collapsed during the Abyssinian Crisis (1935–1936)

Mussolini's invasion of Abyssinia put a huge strain on France's relations with Italy, and, ultimately led to Mussolini withdrawing from the Stresa Front and signing a friendship agreement with Hitler in the Rome-Berlin Axis. This was disastrous from a French perspective and strengthened Hitler's position.

The French government had hoped to steer a middle path through the Abyssinian Crisis, putting enough pressure on Mussolini to get him to withdraw from Abyssinia, and, in so doing, uphold the League of Nations' authority, but without taking action so tough that it would shatter Italy's understanding with France and Britain.

This is best illustrated by the abortive **Hoare-Laval Pact of December 1935**:

- French and British ministers agreed on an offer to Mussolini by which he would receive two-thirds of Abyssinia; news of the secret deal was leaked and led to a political row in both France and Britain, forcing their governments to abandon the plan. However, Mussolini was angered by France and Britain's joining in League sanctions against Italy and by their attempt to deny him the whole of Abyssinia. He turned his back on the democracies and instead signed the Rome-Berlin Axis agreement with Hitler in October 1936.

France's reaction to the *Anschluss* (March 1938)

France, like Britain, protested at the German takeover of Austria but did nothing more, having expected such a move for some time. Furthermore, at the time of the *Anschluss*, France was without a government, with one government having fallen and its replacement not yet in place. The political instability of France in the 1930s was a key factor in its failure to stand up to Hitler until his invasion of Poland.

France's response to the Sudeten Crisis (March–September 1938)

The French government was very alarmed by the deepening political crisis over the Sudetenland, particularly from May 1938 onwards, as it feared that France might get sucked into a war in defence of Czechoslovakia, as it had been a Czech ally since 1924 and had signed another treaty with Czechoslovakia in 1935.

France's military commanders, particularly Gamelin, the Chief of Staff, were extremely pessimistic about the possibility of taking offensive action against Germany, overestimating the strength of Germany's armed forces. France knew that it could not count on Britain for significant help in the event of a war with Germany over Czechoslovakia as Britain could only provide two **divisions** for a continental war. The French cabinet was badly divided over its response to the Sudeten Crisis: Bonnet, the Foreign Minister, was totally opposed to going to war, whereas ministers such as Reynaud favoured strong resistance to German demands over the Sudetenland. Daladier, the Prime Minister, felt caught in the middle, and proved unable to provide strong leadership (Bell, p.271).

Figure 2.13: **Maurice Gamelin, France's Commander-in-Chief, 1936**

Division: a military unit comprising about 10,000 men

This weakness meant that France ended up following Britain's lead, for example, acquiescing in Chamberlain's proposal, following his return from Berchtesgaden (15 September), that Britain and France should press the Czech government to accept the transfer to Germany of those areas of the Sudetenland that voted in favour of union with Germany. However, following Hitler's increased demands at Bad Godesberg (22 September), the French government decided that it had to take action in the event of Germany attacking Czechoslovakia, and, on 26 September, French mobilisation commenced. There is no doubt that the French Prime Minister, Daladier, was relieved that Hitler bowed to pressure to attend a conference at Munich over the Sudetenland on 29 September and that war was thus averted.

5. Italy's response

Tension between Fascist Italy and Nazi Germany (1933–early 1935)

Mussolini seems to have been ambivalent in his attitude to Hitler coming to power. On the one hand, he probably welcomed the accession of a fellow fascist leader and saw the potential for Hitler's likely challenge to the post-war settlement to play to Italy's advantage; but, on the other hand, he was anxious that Hitler might prove a threat to the achievement of his own expansionist goals.

Until 1935–1936, it appeared that Mussolini believed that Italy might gain more from an alignment with Britain and France than as an ally of Germany's, or that his best course of action was to position Italy between Britain and France on the one side and Germany on the other, maximising Italy's diplomatic influence in the process.

The Four-Power Pact (June 1933)

Positioning Italy between the democracies and Germany, and thereby increasing Italy's diplomatic weight, appears to have been Mussolini's motivation in taking the initiative to sponsor a four-power pact between Italy, Germany, France and Britain in June 1933. The signatories agreed to work together within the League of Nations and to collaborate in working towards disarmament. However, the pact was never formally ratified and proved to be, in the words of Graham Ross, *"a diplomatic damp squib."* (Ross, p.85)

There is no doubt that, initially, Mussolini was decidedly suspicious of Hitler. Mussolini's first meeting with Hitler—in Venice in July 1934—was a tense affair. Mussolini wanted Austria as a satellite state of Italy and feared that Hitler would seek to take it over and that he would then demand German-speaking South Tyrol, which Italy had acquired from Austria-Hungary in 1919.

The Dollfuss *Putsch* (July 1934)

In July 1934 Austrian Nazis murdered the Austrian chancellor, Dollfuss, who had close links with Mussolini, but failed to seize power. Mussolini moved Italian troops to the Brenner Pass (the Italian-Austrian border) in order to warn Hitler off intervening in Austria, although it is not clear whether Hitler had been planning an invasion.

The Stresa Front (April 1935)

When Hitler broke the Versailles Treaty in March 1935, by announcing the reintroduction of conscription and his intention to build up an army of 550,000, Mussolini signed the Stresa Front with Britain and France. The three powers agreed to take collective action in the event of any further German breach of Versailles.

The collapse of the Stresa Front and the signing of the Rome-Berlin Axis (1935–1936)

Mussolini invaded Abyssinia in October 1935, expecting Britain and France not to oppose him, but Britain and France condemned this aggression.

During the Abyssinian Crisis, Germany continued to trade with Italy, and Mussolini, angry at Britain and France's attempts to pressurise him into pulling out of Abyssinia, moved to sign the Rome-Berlin Axis agreement with Hitler in October 1936.

This diplomatic realignment made Hitler more confident in looking to make further breaches of the Versailles Treaty, whilst conversely weakening Britain and France's resolve to confront German expansionism.

2. CASE STUDY: GERMAN AND ITALIAN EXPANSION (1933–1940)

2.3 *EVENTS:* **German Expansion (1938–1939); Nazi-Soviet Pact, and the Outbreak of War**

1. **Hitler's seizure of the rest of Czechoslovakia and Memel (March 1939)**

   Chamberlain and Daladier soon discovered that appeasement was based on a fundamental misunderstanding of Hitler's aims: he was not going to be content with the union of all German-speakers.

   Hitler began to encourage the separatist feelings of the Slovaks and growing disorder broke out within Carpatho-Ukraine, leading the Czech President, Hacha, to declare **martial law**. The Slovakian Diet responded by declaring Slovak independence on 14 March, which led Hacha to go to Berlin in a desperate attempt to negotiate a settlement with Hitler (Kitchen, 2006, pp.412–413). Threatened by Hitler with immediate invasion, Hacha gave in and agreed that his country should be further divided up and that the Czech part of it should become part of the Reich.

   Martial law: the use of the military to maintain order, suspension of civil liberties

   On 15 March, the Czech provinces of Bohemia and Moravia were occupied by German troops and became part of Germany. Slovakia was to be an independent state, though the Slovaks had to conduct their foreign policy along lines laid down by Berlin. A week later Hitler successfully demanded that Lithuania hand back Memel, a city with German inhabitants, which Germany had lost as a result of the Versailles Treaty.

2. **The Polish Crisis**

   The German government made a number of approaches to Poland between October 1938 and January 1939. Ribbentrop (German Foreign Minister) proposed to Lipski (Polish ambassador to Germany) that:

   - Danzig, a mainly German-speaking city, should be reincorporated into Germany—it had become a Free City under League control following the First World War but with Poland using its port facilities.
   - Germany should have rail and road access across the 'Polish Corridor', separating East Prussia from the main part of Germany.
   - Poland should sign the Anti-Comintern Pact.
   - Germany would offer Poland a guarantee for its frontier with Germany and the extension of the 1934 Non-Aggression Pact into a 25-year agreement.

   It is possible that Hitler hoped that the Poles would agree to hand over Danzig and then become allies in Germany's planned war against the USSR (Bell, p.292). Jozef Beck, the Polish Foreign Minister, strongly opposed the German proposals and was committed to maintaining Poland's balanced position between the USSR and Germany. To adhere to the Anti-Comintern Pact and concede Danzig to Germany would, Beck believed, risk Poland's subordination to Germany.

   Figure 2.14: **Jozef Beck addressing the Polish Sejm (Parliament), rejecting Hitler's demands, May 1939**

   Hitler repeated Germany's demands to Beck in person when Beck visited Berlin in January 1939 but Beck was evasive. Ribbentrop made a last attempt at gaining

Poland's acquiescence when he visited Warsaw on 26 January but failed to get Polish agreement (Bell, p.292).

The Poles, encouraged by Britain's guarantee, decided to refuse Hitler's demand for Danzig and, in late March, ordered partial mobilisation, which angered Hitler. On 6 April, Germany ended negotiations with Poland, and, on 11 April, Hitler issued a directive for an attack on Poland known as 'Case White.' (Bell, p.299)

Shortly after taking the decision to prepare to invade Poland, Hitler made it clear, in a secret speech to his military commanders, that his motivation stemmed from his overarching racial vision:

> *"A mass of 80 million people [in Germany] has solved the ideological problems. So, too, must the economic problems be solved…The solution of these problems demands courage… This is impossible without invasion of foreign states or attacks upon foreign property.*
> *Living space proportionate to the size of the state is the basis of all power… The choice remains between ascent or decline."*

Mawdsley, p.90

Although Hitler was now intent on war with Poland, he was determined to avoid a general European war for another three or four years *"when the armaments programme will be completed."* At this stage, he knew that Germany was not yet ready economically or militarily for such a conflict. In May, Hitler declared that *"Our task is to isolate Poland…It must not come to a simultaneous showdown with the West."* (Overy, p.55)

Hitler was convinced, following Britain and France's weakness at Munich in September 1938, that neither country would go to war over Poland, denouncing the French and British leaders as *"little worms."* He told the Italian Foreign Minister in August 1939 that *"the conflict will be localised…France and England will certainly make extremely theatrical anti-German gestures but will not go to war."* (Overy, p.55)

Although Hitler was convinced that Britain was bluffing over Poland, he was concerned about the possibility of Britain and France concluding a deal with the USSR in order to safeguard Poland against a German invasion. From March 1939, the German government was aware of secret discussions taking place in Moscow involving British and French delegations. To counter this threat, in August, Hitler secretly approached the Soviet Government for an alliance, which was concluded by Ribbentrop and Molotov on 23 August.

3. **The Nazi-Soviet Pact (23 August 1939)**

This agreement between Fascist Germany and the Communist USSR came as a great shock to the British and French. Stalin was seeking to buy time in which to strengthen his armed forces for the war with Germany, which he believed to be inevitable. The pact also contained a secret agreement in which Russia and Germany would divide up Poland between them and Russia was given permission to seize Estonia, Latvia and certain territories from Finland and Rumania. Poland had been recreated as an independent state in 1919 at the expense of both Germany and Russia, so in one sense the Nazi-Soviet Pact was a delayed response by Poland's powerful neighbours to retrieve the territories they had lost and eliminate Poland in the process.

'Rumania' and 'Romania' were used commonly in the English-speaking world until the mid-20th century, after which 'Romania' became the standard form.

Hitler seems to have been convinced that the pact would deter Britain and France from defending Poland. Germany military planning in August 1939 was directed purely towards a local conflict.

2. CASE STUDY: GERMAN AND ITALIAN EXPANSION (1933–1940)

EXAM PRACTICE 9

Source I: Cartoon printed in *Mucha*, a weekly magazine in Warsaw, on 8 September, 1939. The caption reads: 'The Prussian Tribute in Moscow'

Practice question

For Question 1, part (b):

What is the message conveyed by Source I?
[2 marks]

Figure 2.15: **The Prussian Tribute in Moscow'**

4. **Hitler's invasion of Poland (September 1939)**

On 1 September, 1939, after fabricating a border incident which was blamed on the Poles, Germany invaded Poland. On 3 September, Britain and France declared war on Germany. This action caught Hitler by surprise; his press chief, Otto Dietrich, recalled that *"It was plain to see how stunned he* [Hitler] *was* [by Britain and France's declaration of war]." (Overy, p.60)

The Germans swiftly defeated the Poles. This was due to Germany employing larger forces than Poland (twice the number of troops, four times the number of aircraft and five times as many tanks), the speed and mobility of the German forces (who employed '**Blitzkrieg**' tactics), and mistakes by the Poles—notably their decision to deploy their forces in a long, thin line along their western border (Mawdsley, p.99).

Blitzkrieg: 'lightning war'—characterised by rapid movement of forces, using tanks and aircraft

The Polish forces had effectively already collapsed by 17 September when Soviet troops attacked Eastern Poland. On 27 September, Warsaw surrendered to the German forces encircling it. A week later, the last Polish forces surrendered. On 28 September, Germany and the USSR signed a treaty dividing up Poland between them, with Germany taking control of Poland's territory up to the River Bug. Germany incorporated half of the Polish territory it had acquired in to the German state, with the other half established as the 'General-Government', as a colonial offshoot of Germany. Poland's eastern territories were incorporated by Stalin into the Ukrainian and Belorussian republics within the USSR (Mawdsley, p.101).

Figure 2.16: **Polish infantry marching**

Following Poland's defeat, Hitler hoped to be able to negotiate an agreement with Britain in which Britain accepted Germany's conquest of Poland but Britain refused to do so.

65

2.3.1 RESPONSES: International Response to German Aggression (1939–1940)

The end of appeasement (March 1939)

The Munich Conference marked a watershed for Britain and France in terms of their reactions to Hitler's expansionism because the concessions they had made to Hitler at Munich marked the furthest either country was prepared to go for the sake of preserving peace. P. M. H. Bell points out that the British government:

> "would not buy peace at the price of German domination of Europe and the threat to British interests and independence that that implied, nor would they accept forever methods of unrestrained subversion, bullying and coercion. Hitler's claim that he sought only territory inhabited by German-speaking peoples was accepted, but was regarded as setting a limit in terms of both power and morality. When that limit was overstepped, British policy...would change."

Bell, p.283

Deterrence: discouraging aggressive behaviour by the threat of reprisals

That limit was overstepped by Hitler when he invaded Czechoslovakia in March 1939. Following this, the British government shifted towards a strategy of **deterrence**. Halifax, the British foreign secretary, explained that:

> "Our policy was to resist Germany's attempts at domination...and the best means of stopping German aggression was almost certainly to make it clear that we should resist it by force."

Halifax, cited in Lamb and Tarling, p.143

Britain and France's responses to Germany's invasion of Czechoslovakia (15 March 1939) and incorporation of Memel into Germany (23 March 1939)

Britain and France, as well as the USSR and the US, made formal protests to Germany following Germany's invasion of Czechoslovakia and subsequent incorporation of Bohemia and Moravia into a protectorate of Germany, with Slovakia officially independent but in practice a puppet state of Germany.

15 and 17 March 1939:	**Chamberlain moves from mild to stern protest** Chamberlain's initial statement in the House of Commons on 15 March constituted a very mild protest but, in a second speech in Birmingham, on 17 March, he struck a much tougher tone. This change seems partly to have been a response to demands for tougher action within the Conservative Party and the British press, including *The Times* newspaper, which had previously strongly supported appeasement (Bell, p.294).
31 March:	**Britain guarantees Poland** Neville Chamberlain promised that Britain would defend Poland if its independence was threatened and France joined in this guarantee. Poland appeared likely to be Hitler's next target as, over the winter of 1938–1939, he had demanded that Danzig be handed over to Germany and for German control over rail and road links across the Polish Corridor, linking East Prussia to the main part of Germany; many interpreted this as Hitler seeking a pretext to invade Poland.

2. CASE STUDY: GERMAN AND ITALIAN EXPANSION (1933–1940)

However, Chamberlain's political opponents pointed out that his announcement was a rather vague promise because Chamberlain had not committed Britain to defend Poland's '**territorial integrity**.' Furthermore, the British government was very slow to follow up their guarantee with a military alliance with Poland; this did not happen until August, and, in the meantime, Britain offered just a £5 million loan to Poland for the buying of weapons in response to a Polish request for £60 million (Bell, p.297). France took a similarly lukewarm stance in making good its alliance with Poland and it was clear that neither Britain nor France was prepared to provide direct military assistance to Poland in the event of a German attack. As P. M. H. Bell put it, 'The British and French both hoped that gestures of deterrence would suffice. They would not.' (Bell, p.298)

Territorial integrity: the borders and the land that made up Poland

| April: | **Britain announced conscription for 20–21 year olds** |

This was the first time Britain had had peacetime conscription.

| April–August: | **Anglo-French negotiations for a Soviet Alliance** |

An additional initiative taken by Britain and France in order to deter a German attack on Poland was the opening up of joint Anglo-French negotiations with the USSR for an alliance to defend Poland.

P. M. H. Bell suggests that, "*A firm military alliance between France, Britain and the USSR offered the best, and perhaps the only, chance of confronting Hitler with circumstances in which he would not risk war.*" (Bell, pp.301–302)

The French were keen to secure an alliance with the USSR but Chamberlain was reluctant to enter into negotiations with the Soviet Union. Chamberlain feared that the conclusion of a pact with the USSR would alarm Hitler by appearing to threaten Germany with encirclement and provoke further German aggression. Britain initially proposed that each of the three countries—Britain, France and the USSR—should issue separate guarantees to Poland and Rumania, but the USSR insisted on a treaty providing for joint Anglo-French-Soviet assistance to the states on the USSR's western border.

Under pressure from the French and the Soviets, in late May, the British government accepted the USSR's position. However, it was not until late July that Britain agreed to start military talks and it took until early August for the French and British delegations to arrive in Moscow.

The negotiations proceeded slowly as British officials showed themselves suspicious of the Soviets and progress proved extremely difficult because, on 14 August, Voroshilov, heading the Soviet negotiating team, demanded that Poland would have to agree to Soviet troops entering Poland before a German attack began. The Poles, despite pressure from the French, refused to agree to this demand and the Anglo-French-Soviet talks therefore stalled. Meantime, parallel Soviet-German talks had been taking place but made no progress before August when they accelerated rapidly, resulting in the conclusion of the Nazi-Soviet Pact on 23 August (Bell, pp.301–302).

| July: | **Opinion polls in France and Britain favour going to war in defence of Poland** |

76% of respondents in both countries voted 'yes' in response to the question whether their country should go to war in the event of a German invasion of Poland.

| 25 August: | **Britain formally allied itself to Poland** |

Following Hitler's conclusion of the Nazi-Soviet Pact on 23 August, Hitler appears to have assumed that Britain and France would abandon Poland, but, on 25, August Britain signed a formal alliance with Poland. Chamberlain's government believed that the only way to prevent war was to remain firm in their commitment to defend Poland and, by doing so, deter Hitler.

The French government was divided about whether to honour their alliance with Poland; Prime Minister Daladier was unsure what course to take, whilst Bonnet, the foreign minister, favoured abandoning Poland, and Gamelin, France's commander-in-chief, strongly recommended going to war in the event of Hitler attacking Poland. Reassured by a British commitment to send an expeditionary force to defend France and by information received in late August that Mussolini would not go to war at this point, the French government resolved to go to war if Hitler invaded Poland (R. A. C. Parker, pp.19–20).

The Soviet Union's response to German expansionism in 1939

Some western historians, such as A. J. P. Taylor and Geoffrey Roberts, argue that, in the mid to late 1930s, Stalin tried genuinely to forge a diplomatic and, at times, military front with Britain and France to contain fascism in Europe. They cite, for example, Stalin's joining the League of Nations (1934), the USSR's pact with France and Czechoslovakia (1935), and his aid to the Republicans in the Spanish Civil War (1936–1939), as evidence for this. They argue that Stalin's faith in this policy was shaken by Britain and France's appeasement of Hitler at the Munich Conference in September 1938, to which Stalin was not invited, in spite of his pacts with France and Czechoslovakia. Maxim Litinov, Soviet Foreign Minister 1930–1939, favoured close links with Britain and France but, in May 1939, he was replaced by Vyacheslav Molotov who preferred an agreement with Germany.

Roberts argues that Stalin was genuinely interested in early-mid 1939 in the prospect of an alliance with France and Britain to defend Poland and Rumania against German aggression. He instead puts the blame for the collapse of Soviet-French-British negotiations, and Stalin's subsequent conclusion of the Nazi-Soviet Pact on 23 August, on Britain and France.

In public, the Nazi-Soviet Pact pledged both sides to friendly relations, but there were secret protocols attached to it. In the secret protocols, Stalin and Hitler agreed to partition Poland. In addition, Hitler consented to Soviet expansion at the expense of Latvia, Lithuania, Estonia and Finland.

Why did Stalin agree to the Nazi-Soviet Pact?

1. The Non-Aggression Pact won the USSR a breathing-space; it bought time in which Soviet rearmament could be accelerated and the Red Army officer corps strengthened after Stalin's devastating purges of it during 1937–1938.
2. Stalin could now look to create a buffer zone by expanding into the Baltic States.
3. Stalin presumed that Hitler's planned invasion of Poland would lead to a long drawn-out war between Germany and the western democracies, in which Germany, France and Britain would become exhausted.

Stalin's response to Hitler's invasion of Poland

- Following Hitler's invasion of Poland from the west on 1 September, the USSR invaded Poland from the east on 17 September, acquiring eastern Poland as a result.
- In October 1939, Estonia, Latvia and Lithuania were forced to sign 'mutual assistance' pacts with the USSR, allowing Soviet forces to be based in their countries.
- Stalin demanded that Finland hand over to the USSR a stretch of territory to the west of Leningrad and allow the USSR to use Hanko in southwest Finland as a naval base. After Finland refused, the USSR invaded in November 1939. The Red Army struggled to beat the Finns in the so-called 'Winter War', losing 110,000 soldiers during three months of fighting, but eventually Finland surrendered in March 1940 and was forced to hand over the territories that Stalin had originally demanded. Finland, however, did retain its independence.
- Stalin annexed the three Baltic republics in the summer of 1940 and took Bessarabia from Rumania in June 1940.

2. CASE STUDY: GERMAN AND ITALIAN EXPANSION (1933–1940)

Figure 2.17: **Map showing partition of Poland agreed by Germany and Poland; the map is signed by Stalin and Ribbentrop**

Britain and France's response to Hitler's invasion of Poland

- Two days after Hitler's invasion of Poland on 1 September, Britain and France declared war on Germany. Hitler had probably assumed that France and Britain's guarantees to Poland were just a bluff.
- Britain and France were unable to offer any practical aid to the Poles, who were swiftly defeated by the Germans and by the Russians, who attacked Poland on 17 September. The only offensive action taken by the French was a small-scale advance across the border into the Saar in which they captured a few villages before retreating back into France less than a week later.

Britain and France's response to the fall of Poland (October 1939)

Much to Hitler's surprise, Britain and France refused to accept Germany's occupation of Poland and so Hitler was now committed to a major European war earlier than he had intended. Hitler decided that before he attacked the Soviet Union he must achieve control over Western Europe, so he now resolved on an attack on France, Belgium and Holland, ordering an attack for 12 November 1939, before postponing it for the first of twenty-nine times until it commenced on 10 May 1940.

Britain and France's strategy prior to Hitler's conquest of Poland relied on either delaying any German offensive in the West or, in the event of an attack, holding up the German forces, because they assumed that the balance of economic and military power would tip in their favour as the months passed. Fighting a defensive war initially, Britain and France would build up their military forces to the point where they outnumbered Germany's and could use aerial bombardment and economic blockade to defeat Germany. Germany's swift defeat of Poland and the collaboration between Germany and the USSR meant that Britain and France now realised that a German attack in the West might be imminent, since Hitler could deploy most of his forces for such an assault (Parker, p.23).

In the period between the invasion of Poland and the German attack on France and the Low Countries, Britain and France rapidly accelerated their weapons production,

69

building 1,412 tanks to Germany's 558 in the same period. In the first four months of 1940, Britain and France built 6,794 aircraft, almost twice Germany's production (Parker, p.23).

The 'Phoney War' (October 1939–April 1940)

The six months following Poland's surrender saw no direct fighting between British, French and German forces on land and consequently became known as 'the Phoney War.'

As R. A. C. Parker points out, Britain, following the defeat of Poland, continued to *"have faith in the passive strategy of defence against German attack, and reliance on blockade to make the success of such an attack less and less likely."* (Parker, p.23) However, the French were much less confident about the efficacy of this strategy, and, therefore, put pressure on Britain to agree to a number of offensive options that might weaken Germany's strength for an attack on France. The second and third of the options listed below were designed to reduce the potential for the USSR to be able to provide aid to Germany.

Blockade: preventing goods getting in to a country

The French government tried to persuade Britain to support the following options:

- joint intervention in the Balkans (South-East Europe) to encourage opposition to Germany and Italy from the Balkan states
- allied support for Finland, after it was attacked by the USSR in November 1939, which led to its expulsion from the League of Nations the next month. The Finns eventually surrendered in March 1940, which led to Daladier being replaced as French Prime minister by Reynaud
- allied bombing of Soviet oilfields in the **Caucasus**
- cutting off Germany's iron-ore supplies from Sweden, most of which came through the Norwegian port of Narvik.

Caucasus: a region in the South-West of the USSR

Britain rejected the first three because its government feared that intervention in the Balkans might provoke Mussolini into entering the war against them, whilst the second and third might lead to war with the USSR. The fourth option was delayed by British-French arguments until April 1940.

Germany's invasion of Norway and Denmark (April 1940)

On 8 April, the British navy started laying mines along the coast of Norway but the Germans had already despatched troop ships to Norway and invaded Norway and Denmark on 9 April. So the British and French were confronted with German forces already established in both Norway and Denmark. British-French forces landed in Norway but failed to expel the Germans and withdrew following the German invasion of France. The failure of the Norwegian campaign led to Neville Chamberlain's resignation on 10 May.

Figure 2.18: **German infantry attacking through a burning Norwegian village, April 1940**

Germany's Blitzkrieg against France, Belgium and Holland (May–June 1940)

10 May 1940: On the day that Winston Churchill took over as Prime Minister, the Germans attacked Holland, Belgium, Luxembourg and France. The combined French, British and Belgian forces were roughly equal in numbers and equipment to the Germans as shown

2. CASE STUDY: GERMAN AND ITALIAN EXPANSION (1933–1940)

in the table below, although the German air force had more modern aircraft compared to their opponents who had many obsolete planes.

The strength of the two sides in 1940

	Britain, France and Belgium	Germany
No. of infantry divisions	111	136
No. of troops of the best quality	650,000	1,000,000
No. of tanks	3,200	2,700
No. of aircraft	1,800	3,000

Source: R. A. C. Parker, *The Second World War: A Short History* (1997), pp.28–30

Figure 2.19: **Rotterdam centre after its destruction by German bombers on 14 May, 1940**

Germany's approach to tank warfare

The key to German success in 1940 was based on better strategy and tactics. Crucially, Germany created discrete armoured divisions instead of dispersing their tanks among infantry divisions. The British and French had made the mistake of dispersing their tanks in the First World War and continued, to a large extent, to do so in 1940.

By 1939, German possessed six **Panzer** divisions and, in addition, 4 'light' divisions, which included tanks, making the world's biggest specialised tank force. The key figure in pushing the importance of tank development had been Heinz Guderian. German military planners had originally devised a plan for an invasion of France which had, as its key element, an attack via Belgium, similar to the **Schlieffen Plan**. However, Hitler approved a radically different plan proposed by General Manstein, who, like Guderian, argued that Germany's panzer divisions should be concentrated for a breakthrough at a single point in the Ardennes region, rather than dispersed across a wide front.

Panzer: a model of German tank

Schlieffen Plan: Germany's pre-First World War plan to knock-out France by invading Belgium

HISTORY SL & HL: THE MOVE TO GLOBAL WAR

Anglo-French deployment in 1940

The French and British assumed that the main German attack on France would come through Belgium and Luxembourg, as in 1914. Anglo-French forces facing the Germans in 1940 were deployed across three sectors:

- along the Franco-German border, along the length of the Maginot Line of fortifications up to the Ardennes
- the Ardennes region; but French military planners regarded the area as too hilly and wooded to be suitable for tanks, and so only low calibre reserve troops were deployed to defend it
- along the French-Belgian border, were placed the best French units and the British Expeditionary Force and many of the Anglo-French forces' tanks. The French had decided that, as soon as the German attack began, the Anglo-French forces should advance into Belgium and Holland.

The German Invasion of France

10–13 May 1940	The main German strike force, Army Group A, advanced rapidly through the Ardennes and had crossed the River Meuse by 13 May. Army Group A's mission was, having penetrated the French border, to advance to the coast and isolate Anglo-French forces in Belgium from those in France and trap the former against the sea. The Allies were surprised by both the timing and location of the main German thrust.
20 May	German advance forces reached the Somme estuary on the coast, cutting off French and British forces to the north.
19–25 May	British and French commanders drew up plans for counter-offensives against the Germans from both the north and south but these were abandoned and, on 26 May, the British decided on the evacuation of their forces from Dunkirk.
24–26 May	Hitler halted the panzers' advance towards the Channel because he was worried that the terrain near the coast was not suitable for tanks.
26–28 May	Britain's War Cabinet discussed whether to seek peace terms from Germany and resolved not to.
27 May–4 June	Hitler's halting of the panzers' advance to the Channel gave British commanders time to organise the evacuation of British and French forces at Dunkirk between 27 May and 4 June. Thanks to the 'Miracle of Dunkirk', 338,000 British and French troops were rescued but the British Expeditionary Force had to abandon all of its heavy equipment.
5–14 June	After German forces secured the Channel ports, they turned south to complete the destruction of French units south of the main German breakthrough. Between 5 and 9 June, French forces, totaling 45 divisions, fought bravely to try to hold up 95 advancing German divisions at the rivers Somme and Aisne but the Germans broke through on 9 June and entered Paris on 14 June.
16 June	Reynauld resigned and was replaced as Prime Minister by Pétain, who was known to want peace.
21 June	Pétain's government signed an armistice with Germany. Hitler had succeeded in 1940 where Kaiser Wilhelm II had failed in 1914, defeating France in just six weeks and suffering relatively light casualties (27,000). General Charles de Gaulle escaped to London and led the 'Free French' resistance for the duration of the war.

2. CASE STUDY: GERMAN AND ITALIAN EXPANSION (1933–1940)

The terms that Hitler imposed on France included German occupation of much of northern and western France, including the whole of the Atlantic coastline. Hitler decided to allow 'Vichy' France—Marshal Pétain's government was based in the spa town of Vichy—to retain its colonies in North Africa, which angered Mussolini and ensured that General Franco would not enter the war on Hitler's side, instead remaining neutral.

In explaining the astounding success of the German invasion of France, R. A. C. Parker observes:

> "The unexpected strength of the German forces in an unexpected sector could be countered only by rapid reaction and redeployment by the French. At this stage inferior staff work and inadequacies in the higher commands brought defeat…The best French troops and their equipment and morale were fully equal to those of the best German troops. They were defeated because too often they were not in the right place at the right time."
>
> Parker, pp.33–34

Hitler's spectacular victories left Britain undefeated, although Britain had been forced to evacuate its expeditionary force at Dunkirk. Hitler still hoped for a negotiated peace but Churchill was defiant and Britain fought on. This determination to fight on alone against Germany was brutally demonstrated on 3 July when Churchill ordered the destruction of the French Mediterranean fleet to prevent it from falling into German hands. Thousands of French sailors were killed at Mers-el-Kébir, which led Vichy France to sever diplomatic relations with Great Britain.

Figure 2.20: **Aircraft spotter during the Battle of Britain**

Figure 2.21: **Heinkel He III bombers**

The Battle of Britain (July–September 1940)

Hitler, therefore, decided that he must invade Britain in order to knock her out of the war before turning his attention to the USSR, and, on 2 July, he ordered the drawing up of plans for the invasion of Britain. In order to neutralise the Royal Navy and make possible a sea-borne invasion of Britain, Germany had to achieve air superiority. However, the *Luftwaffe* failed to win control of the skies in the Battle of Britain, which commenced in July 1940 and reached its climax in August–September. The threat of Germany winning control of the skies passed after 7 September when Hitler switched the *Luftwaffe's* main target away from RAF air bases to bombing London. In the battle, the RAF lost 792 planes whilst the *Luftwaffe* lost 1,389 (Parker, p.51). On 12 October, Hitler postponed the invasion

Luftwaffe: German airforce

of Britain until spring 1941, but the plans were then dropped as Hitler focused on invading the USSR.

The US's response to German aggression:

President Roosevelt was sympathetic towards Britain as British forces fought on alone against Hitler, but was conscious that most Americans were strongly in favour of remaining neutral in the war. In November 1939, Congress did amend the Neutrality Acts to allow countries at war to purchase weapons from the US provided they could pay for and transport them. Britain placed very large aircraft and weapons orders with American factories. In the second half of 1940, over half of Britain's imports came from the US and Canada.

Figure 2.22: **President Roosevelt signing the Lend-lease Bill, May 1941**

Roosevelt did provide some direct help to Britain, agreeing in September 1940 to give Britain fifty old **destroyers** in return for Britain allowing the US to lease air and naval bases in the West Indies and Newfoundland. However, it was not until March 1941 and Congress' Lend-Lease Act, that the US provided Britain with aid without payment—up until that point, Britain had had to pay for everything she got from the US (Parker, pp.57–58).

Destroyer: a type of warship used in World War II

2.4   EVENTS: Italian Expansion: Abyssinia (1935–1936)

The Abyssinian War of 1935–1936 was a key turning point, both in the fortunes of the League of Nations and in Mussolini's foreign policy; as a result of the invasion, his relations with Britain and France deteriorated and he drew closer to Hitler's Germany. The League's authority, already undermined by its failure in the Manchurian Incident, was further weakened.

Note that some texts refer to Abyssinia as 'Ethiopia'

What were Mussolini's aims in invading Abyssinia?

1. to link up Italy's existing colonies in North-East Africa (Eritrea and Italian Somaliland); to create a greater East African empire
2. to gain revenge for the Italian defeat by the Abyssinians at Adowa in 1896
3. to satisfy the many Italian nationalists who had been angry at Italy's failure to acquire any colonies as a result of the 1919–1920 peace settlement
4. to be able to claim to be recreating the glories of the ancient Roman Empire in North Africa.

The Italian historian, Carocci, presents Mussolini's invasion of Abyssinia as a search by Mussolini for a way out of domestic difficulties:

> "People all over the country felt indifferent to the regime, detached from it. In order to overcome these feelings, in order to galvanise the masses and try to break the vicious circle of economic crisis, more drastic and more attractive measures were needed."
>
> Quoted in Lee (1987), p.125

On the other hand, historians such as MacGregor Knox, see Mussolini's motivation as primarily ideological—viewing the invasion as Mussolini's pursuit of *spazio vitale* ('living space').

Why did Mussolini believe that Britain and France would permit his invasion of Abyssinia?

Mussolini believed that France and Britain would not take any action against Italy if it invaded Abyssinia because:

1. Pierre Laval, the French Foreign Minister, had, in January 1935, agreed that there were no major French interests at stake in Abyssinia.
2. in April 1935, Britain and France had signed the Stresa Front agreement with Mussolini; under its terms, the three countries agreed to take co-ordinated action against any country unilaterally violating existing treaties.

At this stage, Mussolini was very suspicious of Hitler's foreign ambitions and was anxious that they might conflict with Italy's influence over Austria and his own ambitions to expand into the Balkans. The British and French governments were very keen to maintain a common front with Mussolini and to use it as a deterrent against further German breaches of the Versailles Treaty. The Stresa Front, therefore, conditioned to a considerable extent British and French policies towards the Abyssinian Crisis as they did not want the crisis to jeopardise their agreement with Mussolini.

- In June 1935, Anthony Eden, a British minister, visited Rome and proposed a deal between Abyssinia and Italy which would have given Italy the Ogaden region and compensated Abyssinia with a piece of British Somaliland, allowing Abyssinia access to the sea.

The Wal-Wal Incident (December 1934)

Mussolini was certainly considering an attack on Abyssinia from 1932 onwards, if not before. He picked a quarrel with Abyssinia after a small military clash at Wal-Wal in December 1934.

Abyssinia referred the Wal-Wal incident to the League of Nations. Although it is clear that Mussolini was now intent on an invasion of Abyssinia, he agreed to League of Nations' arbitration over the incident. However, in the meantime, Mussolini built up forces in preparation for an invasion, shipping and airlifting large numbers of troops to Italy's possessions in Libya and Eritrea. The League's arbitration committee did not produce its report until September 1935 and did not reach a clear conclusion.

Wal-Wal: an oasis town in Abyssinia (or Ethiopia as it is now known) close to the border with Somalia. In 1934, Italian troops based in Somalia crossed into Abyssinia and clashed with Abyssinian troops at Wal-Wal.

Mussolini's invasion of Abyssinia (October 1935)

Italian troops, tanks and planes invaded from Eritrea to the north. Before the invasion, Emperor Haile Selassie of Abyssinia had appealed four times to the League of Nations for help but the League of Nations took no action until war began.

Contrary to Mussolini's expectations, the League of Nations imposed economic sanctions on Italy following its invasion of Abyssinia in October 1935. Mussolini completed the conquest of Abyssinia in May 1936. Emperor Haile Selassie went into exile.

Figure 2.23: **Haile Selassie making a radio broadcast**

2.4.1 RESPONSES: International Response to Italian Aggression (1935–1936)

The League of Nations' Response

Contrary to Mussolini's expectations, in early October 1935, both the League Council and the Assembly condemned Italy's invasion and 50 of the 54 Assembly members voted in favour of economic sanctions. This was largely because the British government took a lead as it felt under pressure from public opinion—which evidently was very pro-League, as demonstrated by the **Peace Ballot** organised by the League of Nations Union in June 1935—to take a stand against Italy. The 50 Assembly members then set up a committee and then a sub-committee of 18 to consider how to apply sanctions.

The League sub-committee on sanctions produced recommendations which eventually were implemented on 18 November:

- Sales of arms, rubber and certain metals to Italy were banned.
- Loans to Italy were banned.
- Most Italian imports were also banned.

Sanctions, however, did not prove effective, partly because they were not introduced until 18 November, six weeks after Mussolini began his invasion. In addition, they did not include some of the very materials that Mussolini needed most, particularly oil, iron, steel and coal. This reflected the dilemma that the League's leading powers, Britain and France, found themselves in: they wanted to apply sufficient pressure on Mussolini to resolve the Abyssinian Crisis but not so much that it led Mussolini to break off relations with them.

A further limitation concerning the efficacy of sanctions was that countries who were not League members, such as the US, Germany and Japan, continued to trade with Italy. Furthermore, sanctions took some time to have a significant impact on Italy; not until early 1936 was the Italian economy really affected adversely. The sub-committee of 18, in January 1936, established an expert group to look into the option of a ban on oil sales to Italy. The experts reported back in February that a ban on oil exports to Italy would have a significant effect within 3 to 4 months, but only if the US participated in such an embargo (and this was a very remote possibility).

> **Peace Ballot**: A nationwide referendum held in Britain in 1934, with the results announced in June 1935. People were asked 5 questions about their attitudes to the League of Nations and collective security. Eleven million people took part and their responses overwhelmingly supported Britain's membership of the League of Nations, collective security, and multilateral disarmament.

2. CASE STUDY: GERMAN AND ITALIAN EXPANSION (1933–1940)

The imposition of sanctions—even though oil and steel were not included—angered Mussolini. Germany ignored the sanctions and continued to trade with Italy. US oil exports to Italy continued during the Abyssinian Crisis, whilst Rumania increased its oil supplies to Italy from 31% of Italy's total oil imports in 1934 to 59% in 1935–1936 (Overy, p.164).

Britain and France could have applied much greater pressure on Mussolini by closing the **Suez Canal**—which they owned—to Italian supply ships, forcing them to re-route thousands of kilometres around Africa but decided against this action.

Suez Canal: the British and French owned waterway opened in 1869 connecting the Mediterranean and Red seas.

Why were Britain and France not prepared to take tougher action against Mussolini?

1. They feared Hitler and desperately wanted to keep the two fascists dictators apart (as shown by the Stresa Front of 1935).
2. Britain and France were very keen to avoid war with Italy because they had not properly rearmed since the end of the First World War and were worried about the threat posed to their Far Eastern colonies by the Japanese.

The Hoare-Laval Pact (December 1935)

Sir Samuel Hoare (Britain) and Pierre Laval (France) reached a secret agreement in Paris that two-thirds of Abyssinia should be offered to Italy, and the Emperor Haile Selassie be compensated with land elsewhere instead. However, news of the proposed pact leaked out and there was a huge public outcry in both France and Britain. Both politicians lost their jobs as a result.

Mussolini completed the conquest of Abyssinia in May 1936. The League of Nations ended its sanctions on Italy in July 1936.

What were the results of the Abyssinian War?

1. **Internationally:**
   - The Stresa Front between Italy, Britain and France, already weakened by the Anglo-German Naval Convention, collapsed.
   - Mussolini drew closer to Hitler, whose own aggression was encouraged by Mussolini's flouting of the League. In October 1936, Hitler and Mussolini signed the Rome-Berlin Axis, a friendship and trade agreement.
   - Hitler re-occupied the Rhineland in March 1936, exploiting the fact that international attention was focused on the Abyssinian Crisis.
   - Mussolini undermined the League of Nations and withdrew Italy from membership of it.
   - The successful conquest of Abyssinia also made Mussolini more open to take risks and use force.

2. **For Italy:**
   - The war was very popular in Italy.
   - Abyssinia did not prove of significant commercial value to Italy; in 1939 only 2% of Italy's trade was with Abyssinia.
   - Sanctions hurt the Italian economy.
   - The war was very expensive, costing 40 million lire, and Italian troops were engaged in fighting Abyssinian guerrillas until 1939.

Figure 2.24: **Mussolini cheered by Fascist Youth in Rome, 1935**

2.5 EVENTS: Italian Intervention in the Spanish Civil War (1936)

Both Mussolini and Hitler intervened in the Spanish Civil War, which broke out in July 1936, in support of General Franco's Nationalists' rebellion against the Republican government. Mussolini's decision seems to have been spontaneous and, in contrast to the invasion of Abyssinia, there was no prior detailed planning (Overy, p.165).

Mussolini sent 70,000 troops to Spain, but they performed poorly, suffering a humiliating defeat at Guadalajara in March 1937, where Italian anti-fascists formed part of the opposing force.

Why did Mussolini intervene in Spain?
1. Mussolini wanted to weaken France, which had a left-wing Popular Front government similar to the Spanish government, by installing a right-wing regime in Spain, which he hoped would become a satellite state of Italy.
2. He also wanted to acquire naval bases in the Balearic Islands, which would help promote Italian power in the Mediterranean.

However, Mussolini gained very little from intervention in Spain, which proved very costly (14 million lire).

2. CASE STUDY: GERMAN AND ITALIAN EXPANSION (1933–1940)

2.6 EVENTS: Mussolini Establishes Closer Relations with Nazi Germany

October 1936	Italy and Germany signed the Rome-Berlin Axis, a commercial and friendship treaty.
September 1937	Mussolini visited Germany and was received very warmly by Hitler.
November 1937	Italy signed the Anti-Comintern Pact (originally signed by Germany and Japan in 1936).
December 1937	Italy walked out of the League of Nations, as Germany had done back in 1933.
March 1938	Mussolini signalled his approval prior to Hitler's invasion of Austria. As, from 1936 onwards, Mussolini drew closer to Hitler, he changed his policy towards Austria and decided to allow Hitler to increase German influence over Austria. In January 1936, Mussolini told Hitler that he was happy for Austria to become a client state of Germany. In March 1938, Hitler felt compelled to organise an immediate takeover of Austria after the Austrian chancellor, Schuschnigg, announced that he would call a referendum on Austria's independence. Hitler contacted Mussolini immediately before invading Austria to check that he would not object—Mussolini duly gave his approval.
November 1938	Probably in an attempt to cement his friendship with Hitler, Mussolini introduced a series of **anti-semitic** laws in Italy. There is no doubt that many radical fascists saw the German alliance as a way of radicalising the Fascist regime in Italy. Mussolini himself certainly came to fall under Hitler's spell.

Anti-semitic: anti-Jewish

Historians dispute the causes of the Italian-German rapprochement, with Knox arguing that it stemmed from shared ideological positions, whilst Overy takes a different approach.

Figure 2.25: **Mussolini and Hitler in Munich in September 1938**

Source J: Richard Overy's assessment of the reasons behind the Italian-German alliance from *The Road to War* (p.169):

> The fact that they were both fascist powers gave the relationship a gloss of ideological brotherhood and dictatorial solidarity, but co-operation between them was always more cautious and formal. Italy was useful to Hitler as a fascist outpost in the Mediterranean keeping Britain and France away from Central Europe. Germany was useful to Mussolini as a source of economic assistance for rearmament, and as a power to divert the attention of Britain and France from Italian adventures in the Mediterranean. Each saw the other as an instrument in his own power game: manipulation rather than friendship bound them together.

Practice question

For Question 1, part (a):

Why according to Source J did Italy and Germany become allies? [3 marks]

2.7 *EVENTS*: The Sudeten Crisis and the Munich Conference (1938)

In 1938, a crisis broke out over Hitler's demand that the Czech government allow the German-speaking area of Czechoslovakia—the Sudetenland—to unite with Germany. By September 1938, it looked likely that Germany would invade Czechoslovakia and that Britain and France might then intervene on the Czechs' side. War was averted when Mussolini helped set up the Munich Conference in September 1938. Mussolini was keen to avoid war breaking out and was able to pose as a mediator between Hitler and the British and French.

Mussolini was encouraged by Britain and France's appeasement of Hitler over the Sudetenland (and the *Anschluss*), to believe that neither country would stand up to aggression and this, in part, explains Mussolini's increasingly belligerent foreign policy from the late 1930s onwards.

Mussolini was very much aware of the fact that Italy was the junior partner in the Italian-German relationship, as evidenced by Hitler's failure to inform Mussolini before he occupied the rest of Czechoslovakia in March 1939; this became increasingly the case in the period 1939–1943 and was one reason for Mussolini's determination to increase Italy's influence and possessions by force. In February 1939, Mussolini announced to the Fascist Grand Council his intention that Italy should break out of the 'prison' of the Mediterranean. He said that the 'bars' of the prison were "*Corsica, Tunisia, Malta and Cyprus; its sentinels Gibraltar and Suez* [all possessions of either France or Britain]." (Knight, p.97)

2. CASE STUDY: GERMAN AND ITALIAN EXPANSION (1933–1940)

2.8 EVENTS: The Invasion of Albania (7 April 1939)

To an extent, the invasion by Italian troops was a publicity stunt by Mussolini as Albania was already virtually under Italian control, with Ahmed Zogu (King Zog) seen as a client of Mussolini's and Italy having established a semi-protectorate over Albania in 1927. Mussolini wanted to show that he had made some gains following on Germany's expansion in 1938–1939 and the invasion of Albania was probably a hastily improvised response to Hitler's invasion of Czechoslovakia three weeks earlier. Aristotle A. Kallis (2000) suggests that the invasion of Albania was *"clearly timed by the Italian government to balance the successes of Nazi expansionism in the wider central European area and to block further German intervention in the Balkan sphere."*

Albania was strategically important to Mussolini because of its position at the entrance to the Adriatic. In June 1939, Ciano, Mussolini's foreign minister, stated that following the successful absorption of Albania, Italy needed to break apart Yugoslavia, take all of Dalmatia and create for Italy *"a territorial continuity as far as Albania."* In August 1939, Mussolini ordered his military planners to prepare for an attack on Greece launched from Albania (Kallis, p.133).

2.8.1 RESPONSES: France and Britain's Response to Italy's Invasion of Albania

On 13 April, both France and Britain announced they were guaranteeing Greece and Rumania in the event of either country being attacked. The French took the lead in this initiative, seeking to deter Mussolini from trying to expand further into the Mediterranean. The guarantee to Rumania followed on reports that Hitler intended to subordinate Rumania to German economic control. Both the British and French governments were alarmed at the prospect of Hitler acquiring control over Romania's oil supplies.

2.9 EVENTS: The Pact of Steel (May 1939)

Mussolini fatally tied Italy to Nazi Germany by signing a military alliance, which obliged both countries to support each other in the event of a war. The pact worked to Germany's advantage because it was much more likely that Germany would go to war. Mussolini probably hoped to acquire German support for Italian expansion in the Balkans, Mediterranean and North Africa. The alliance was widely unpopular in Italy as Mussolini's secret police noted growing hostility to Nazi Germany and to Mussolini's increasingly close relationship with Hitler. The closer relationship between the two countries was accompanied by Mussolini's introduction of anti-semitic laws in Italy in 1938; this may well have been motivated by Mussolini's desire to curry favour with Hitler. Certainly the legislation proved deeply unpopular among Italians.

The Pact of Steel was presented in public as the result of a shared ideological perspective:

> *"Closely bound together through internal relationships of ideologies and through comprehensive solidarity of interests, the German and Italian peoples have decided in the future to stand side by side and with united strength in order to secure their living space..."*
>
> Elizabeth Wiskemann, p.413

Philip Morgan argues that, although there was a degree of continuity between Mussolini's foreign policy prior to his invasion of Abyssinia and Italy's pre-First World War foreign policy, there was always a more radical and aggressive element to Mussolini's. Morgan suggests that the changed international landscape of the 1930s, following the onset of the Great Depression and the rise of Hitler, and the diplomatic realignment brought about by the Abyssinian Crisis, both encouraged Mussolini to be less restrained in pursuing his expansionist aims and brought into sharper relief the similar ideological positions of Mussolini and Hitler.

> "Mussolini wanted Italy to be the Mediterranean power, and this could only be achieved at the expense of French and British power and influence in the Mediterranean area. These were ambitions beyond Italy's capacity to realise alone; there was a certain logic, then, in Mussolini allying his country with the most powerful and expansionist power on the continent of Europe, Germany. So the Ethiopian war of 1935–6 was the occasion for a merging of aims and interests between Fascist Italy and Nazi Germany. Both wanted to revise the 1919 settlement, both wanted to expand their territory and power, and both were united together in hostility to France and Britain, the defenders of the 1919 settlement standing in the way of them achieving their goals. By the late 1930s, Mussolini was no more a 'normal' Italian statesman than Hitler was a 'normal' German statesman."
>
> Morgan, pp.68–69

The Ethiopian war of 1935–36 is also known as the Abyssinian Crisis.

However, at this stage, Mussolini had no intention of going to war as he knew how unprepared Italy's armed forces were. It seems that, in signing the Pact of Steel, he assumed that Hitler had no intention of going to war prior to 1943 at the earliest, and, therefore, was totally unprepared for Hitler's invasion of Poland.

Mussolini declares 'non-belligerency' at the outbreak of World War Two (September 1939)

Non-belligerency: not involved in the fighting

Mussolini was very alarmed when he heard in August of Hitler's plans to invade Poland. When Hitler invaded Poland in September and Britain and France declared war, Mussolini announced that Italy was a 'non-belligerent power.' Mussolini told Hitler that he could only enter the war if he received 17,000 trains-full of munitions from Germany, an impossible demand.

The State of Italy's Armed Forces in 1940

Mussolini's dependence on his German ally in the Second World War was largely the result of Italy's continuing economic weakness and lack of raw materials. During the Second World War, this was worsened by Italian imports being disrupted.

Despite Mussolini spending 11.8% of Italy's national income on rearmament in the years 1935–1938, compared to 6.9% in France and 5.5% in Britain, there was not much to show for this investment as much of the spending went on inferior quality weapons.

What evidence is there of Italy's military weakness in 1940?

Italian army	• Mussolini boasted of an army of 8 million but, in 1939, only 0.8 million troops were available. • The Army had only 1,500 tanks (and most of them were light).
Italian navy	• The Italian Navy had no aircraft carriers and only 8 battleships. • Italy did have a large submarine fleet, but a third of its submarines were destroyed by the British in the first 3 weeks of the war.
Italian air force	• The Italian air force lacked long-range bombers and its fighters were slow. • In 1939, Italy had 1500 aircraft compared to Germany's 4,200.

2.10 EVENTS: Italy's Entry into the Second World War (10 June 1940)

Mussolini kept out of the war for the first ten months, torn between a desire to share in any spoils won by Germany and a realisation that Italy was not ready for war. Mussolini was not comfortable with his position of 'non-belligerency' (as he put it) as it was reminiscent of Italy's stance at the start of the First World War.

After Hitler's swift conquest of Poland, Norway, Denmark, Holland and Belgium in September 1939–June 1940 and, with France on the point of collapse, Mussolini decided to declare war. Mussolini was keen not to lose out on any possible territorial gains. Italy declared war on France just two weeks before it surrendered.

Ciano (Mussolini's son-in-law and foreign minister), King Victor Emmanuel, and most of the Italian people were against

Figure 2.26: **Mussolini delivering his declaration of war speech, from the balcony of the Palazzo Venezia in Rome**

Mussolini's decision. Italian forces performed very poorly in the 11 days left of the French campaign before France's surrender on 21 June. Mussolini had declared war before France's defeat in the hope of gaining territory from France in the shape of French colonies but he was to be disappointed in this respect because Hitler wanted to preserve good relations with the new Vichy French government. However, Mussolini went to war also in order to gain territory in the Balkans at the expense of Yugoslavia and Greece and to wrest control of Egypt from Britain.

HISTORY SL & HL: THE MOVE TO GLOBAL WAR

There has been a fierce historiographical debate about Mussolini's entry into the Second World War, which Aristotle A. Kallis helpfully summarises in the following terms:

> "The eventual decision to declare war, according to Renzo De Felice and Giorgio Rochat, entailed a 'modest commitment,' underpinned by the belief in a short war and a swift, 'better peace.' A similar conclusion was reached by Denis Mack Smith, who saw Italy's entry into the war as a diplomatic move and not a real military commitment to large-scale expansion and war-making. By contrast, Knox interpreted Mussolini's path to war as the culmination of an increasingly aggressive expansionist strategy since 1938. According to him, the Duce's references in May 1939 to the unavoidable showdown with the West should be taken at face value instead of being dismissed as mere bluff. Similarly, Altari viewed the same decision as the logical conclusion of Mussolini's overall expansionist strategy since 1935, while Rumi maintained that it stemmed from his vast geopolitical ambitions in the Mediterranean and was not simply dictated by the dynamism of Nazi expansionism."

Kallis, pp.168–169

2.11 EVENTS and RESPONSES: Italian Aggression in 1940–1941; Britain's and Germany's Responses

Italian campaigns in the Balkans and North Africa (1940–1941)

Mussolini wanted to conduct his own campaigns, separate from Hitler's, so he invaded Egypt and Greece in September/October 1940.

September 1940:	Italian forces in Libya invaded Egypt but were driven out by British troops. The Germans had to send troops in and took control of the North African campaign.
October 1940:	Italian troops based in Albania invaded Greece but were quickly expelled by the Greeks. Britain responded to Mussolini's aggression by sending military supplies to Greece along with British troops early in 1941, basing a British bomber force in northern Greece (Ross, p.132).
November 1940:	The Royal Air Force destroyed half of the Italian fleet at Taranto.
February 1941:	Hitler sent Rommel to command German forces dispatched to Libya to bolster Italian forces.
March 1941:	British forces, largely drawn from the British Empire, and supported by Ethiopian fighters, expelled Italian troops from East Africa.
April 1941:	Hitler sent German forces into Yugoslavia and Greece, quickly gaining control of both countries and driving out British troops who had been sent to Greece ahead of the German invasion. In May, German paratroopers captured Crete, driving out British troops stationed there. Greece was then occupied by German and Italian forces. Yugoslavia was divided up: Italy and Bulgaria were given some territory, a separate Croatian state was set up, and, what was left of Yugoslavia was placed under a pro-German government (Ross, pp.132–133).

2. CASE STUDY: GERMAN AND ITALIAN EXPANSION (1933–1940)

Figure 2.27: **Ethiopian men gather, with captured Italian weapons, to hear the announcement of Emperor Haile Selassie's return in May 1941**

2.12 Suggested Points for Exam Practice Questions on Italian and German Expansion

On Source E on page 40:

For Question 2:

With reference to its origins, purpose and content, analyse the value and limitations of Source E for a historian studying Mussolini's foreign policy. [4 marks]

- **Origins**: It is Mussolini's speech announcing Italy's entry in to the Second World War in June 1940. *Value*: It shows how Mussolini personally, and in public, explained why Italy was going to war.

- **Purpose**: It was designed to rally support for the war among Italians. *Limitation*: Mussolini is trying to justify the decision to go to war, so he is presenting it in as positive a light as possible; in doing so, he is hiding the deep divisions within his government about this decision.

- **Content**: It provides an insight into Mussolini's motivation, suggesting a mixture of geopolitical factors (desire to expand Italian influence in the Mediterranean) and ideology (stemmed from the fascist revolution), pitted young, dynamic peoples (Italy, Germany) against old, sterile ones (Britain, France). *Limitation*: It provides no details about specific Italian objectives in going to war; it is couched in very generalised terms.

On Source F on page 42:

For Question 2:

With reference to its origins, purpose and content, analyse the value and limitations of Source F for a historian studying Hitler's foreign policy. [4 marks]

- **Origins**: It is Hitler's autobiography, which published in 1925. *Value*: It provides an insight into Hitler's thinking on foreign policy well before he came to power, and, additionally, a long-term perspective on the motivation that lay behind his foreign policy in the 1930s. **Limitation**: This may not reflect Hitler's thinking in the 1930s, which may have changed significantly.

▶ Purpose: Its purpose was to publicise his views on foreign policy and promote support for the Nazi party. **Limitation**: Hitler might have exaggerated the difference between his foreign policy objectives and that of previous/other parties in order to maximise support.

▶ Content: It outlines the differences between his policy and that of previous German governments, arguing that Germany should turn its back on colonies and instead focus on expansion in to Eastern Europe. *Value*: It indicates that from an early stage Hitler's foreign policy was based on a radical vision of dominating Eastern Europe, different from that of previous German governments and other German parties.

On Source G on page 45:

For Question 1, part (a):

What according to Source G was the impact of the Great Depression on international relations? [3 marks]

- It soured international relations because countries, in putting their own economies first, took measures that antagonised other countries.
- It acted as a catalyst, inflaming existing tensions between countries that in some cases had lain beneath the surface in better economic times in the 1920s.
- Some of those countries worst affected turned to political extremism and this gave rise to aggressive nationalist policies.

On Source H on page 56:

For Question 1, part (a):

How far, according to Source H, did British foreign policy change in the 1930s? [3 marks]

- It didn't change that much because British foreign policy had from the 1920s accepted that the Treaty of Versailles needed changing; *therefore*,
- the appeasement of the mid to late 1930s under Chamberlain was based on policies pursued in the 1920s; *however*,
- in the 1930s British politicians believed that Versailles needed changing faster and further and with Britain playing a greater role in that process.

On Source I on page 65:

For Question 1, part (b):

What is the message conveyed by Source I? [2 marks]

- The USSR was the dominant partner in the Nazi-Soviet Pact with Ribbentrop (Hitler's foreign minister) kneeling before Stalin and paying him 'tribute.'
- Stalin and Molotov were pleased with what they got out of the pact with Germany: both are seen smiling as Ribbentrop kneels with a copy of the agreement in his hand.

2. CASE STUDY: GERMAN AND ITALIAN EXPANSION (1933–1940)

On Source J on page 80:

For Question 1, part (a):

Why according to Source J did Italy and Germany become allies? [3 marks]

- There was an ideological bond between them, but this was essentially superficial, a mere 'gloss' for other more pragmatic reasons.
- Hitler found it convenient to have a close relationship with Italy because Mussolini could distract France and Britain's attention away from German expansion in central Europe.
- Mussolini welcomed the opportunity for economic assistance from Hitler and saw Hitler's expansionism as welcome because it distracted Britain and France away from Mussolini's projected expansion in to the Mediterranean.

2.13 A Complete Set of Practice Source-based Questions: The Abyssinian Crisis

Source A: Anthony Eden (British Foreign Secretary at the time of the Abyssinian Crisis), writing in his autobiography, *Facing the Dictators*, (London, 1962).

I reported the government's opinion that the best action to take would be the **prohibition** of the import of Italian goods. The object of this ban was to deprive Italy of a large part of her power to buy goods abroad. If all members of the league applied this **embargo**, 70 per cent of Italy's export trade would be cut off. Britain now had taken a decision, as one of the fifty nations, to try to stop Mussolini.

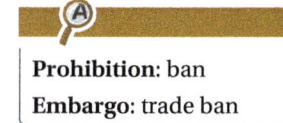

Prohibition: ban
Embargo: trade ban

Source B: Giampiero Carocci, an Italian historian, writing in an academic book, *Italian Fascism*, (Rome, 1972).

In spite of opposition, led by Britain in the League of Nations, Mussolini got everything he wanted: Ethiopia and the Empire. But the most important of the economic sanctions, the one on petrol, was not applied, nor was the Suez Canal closed to Italian ships.

The British government wished to avoid war with Italy at all costs because of the weakness of the British navy after years of disarmament. This weakness made such a war seem completely out the question. Although the British would certainly have won, they would have had to fight without the support of France, and would have been further weakened in the face of two other threats, considered far more serious: Japan and Germany. Through his secret services Mussolini knew how weak the British navy had become and he exploited this knowledge to the full.

Source C: A cartoon published in the British newspaper, the *Daily Dispatch*, December 1935, depicting Mussolini as a child sitting on the lap of a nurse [the League of Nations]

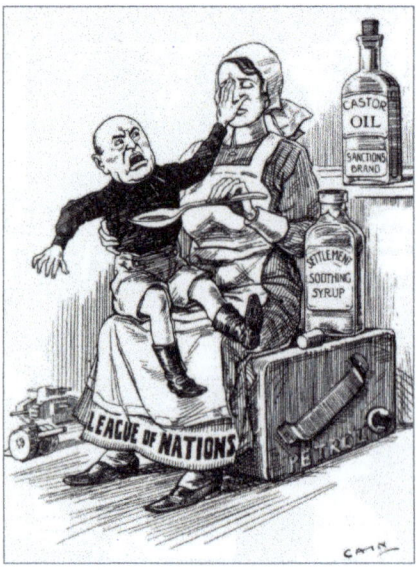

Figure 2.28: **A cartoon in the Daily Dispatch, December 1935**

Source D: Sir Samuel Hoare, the British Foreign secretary, addressing the League of Nations on 2 November 1935.

On 18 November all exports from Italy to those members of the League participating in sanctions will cease...

I will only add that it is with great regret that we have been forced to take this action. We felt, however, that for those of us determined to uphold the principles of the Covenant and collective security, no other course is possible...

I have listened with great sympathy...to the words uttered by Monsieur Laval. He has accurately expressed what is in the minds of all of us. On the one hand, as loyal members of the League, we feel it our bounden duty to carry out the obligations imposed on us by the Covenant. On the other hand, we are under a no less insistent obligation to strive for a speedy settlement of the controversy. It is common talk that there have been conversations taking place between Rome, Paris and London on the possibilities of such a settlement. There is nothing mysterious or sinister about these discussions. It is the duty of all of us to explore the road of peace...Up to the present, the conversations have been nothing more than an exchange of tentative suggestions...

2.13.1 Questions

1. (a) Why according to Source B did Mussolini not need to take seriously the threat of British opposition to his invasion of Abyssinia? [3 marks]

    (b) What is the message of Source C? [2 marks]

2. With reference to its origins, purpose and content, analyse the value and limitations of Source A for a historian studying the Abyssinian Crisis. [4 marks]

3. Compare and contrast what Sources B and D reveal about the British government's policy towards Mussolini's invasion of Abyssinia. [6 marks]

4. Using the sources and your own knowledge, analyse the reasons for the League of Nations' failure to get Mussolini to end his invasion of Abyssinia. [9 marks]

2. CASE STUDY: GERMAN AND ITALIAN EXPANSION (1933–1940)

2.13.2 Mark Scheme

1. (a) Why according to Source B did Mussolini not need to take seriously the threat of British opposition to his invasion of Abyssinia? [3 marks]

   - Mussolini had secret intelligence about the British government and knew it was desperate to avoid war with Italy.
   - Britain had only just started to rearm.
   - He knew that Britain prioritised the Japanese and German threats over the threat posed by Italy.
   - He knew that Britain was not prepared to fight without French support.

   Award [1 mark] for each valid point up to a maximum of [3 marks].

   (b) What is the message of Source C? [2 marks]

   - that the League of Nations [the nurse] is imposing unpalatable sanctions [castor oil] on Italy [the child Mussolini] in an attempt to stop his aggression against Abyssinia [shown by the tank and artillery on the floor]
   - that Mussolini is continuing to behave aggressively [putting his hand over the nurse's face; his angry expression]
   - that the League [nurse] is sitting on the most important commodity, oil; this may imply that the League is not sanctioning this item.

   Award [1 mark] for each relevant point up to a maximum of [2 marks].

2. With reference to its origins, purpose and content, analyse the value and limitations of Source A for a historian studying the Abyssinian Crisis. [4 marks]

Source A

Origin:

- It is the autobiography of Anthony Eden, foreign secretary during the later part of the Abyssinian Crisis, published in London, 1962. Therefore, *Value*: It provides an informed insight into British policy on Abyssinia by a key participant. *Limitation*: It only provides a British perspective on the crisis, not a wider international perspective.

Purpose:

- Its purpose is to explain to the public his part in Britain's foreign affairs, and to justify his (the British government's) conduct. Therefore, *Limitation*: It may distort Britain's/Eden's role in an attempt to justify Britain's stance in a crisis which ended in aggression going unpunished.

Content:

- *Value*: Eden provides an insight into why Britain and the League placed an embargo on Italian exports: to reduce Italy's buying power so that it could not purchase what it needed. He does point out that this would only be effective if all members applied this properly. *Limitations*: Eden does not explain the League's sanctions in terms of banning the export of certain materials (but not oil) to Italy. It only provides an insight into one aspect of the crisis, namely, the decision to embargo Italian exports, and not into other aspects, e.g. the Hoare-Laval Pact.

The IBO's mark scheme advises the following for Question 2:

The focus of the question is on the value and limitations of the source. If *only* value *or* limitations are discussed, award a maximum of [2]. Origin, purpose and content should be used as supporting evidence to make relevant comments on the value and limitations. For [4] there must be at least one reference to each of them in *either* the value *or* the limitations.

3. Compare and contrast what Sources B and D reveal about the British government's policy towards Mussolini's invasion of Abyssinia. [6 marks]

For comparison

- They both discuss Britain's involvement, as part of the League, in enforcing sanctions on Italy.
- They both suggest Britain was reluctant to impose sanctions rigorously (B—sanctions on petrol not applied, nor Suez Canal closed; D—Britain had voted for sanctions with great regret, no reference by Hoare to banning exports to Italy).
- They both refer to the British government's desire to avoid a war/reach a peaceful settlement.
- They both suggest France's attitude in the crisis was an important influence on British policy.

For contrast

- Source B suggests that Britain wanted to avoid war with Italy at all costs, whereas Source D suggests that, although Britain wanted a peaceful settlement, it would uphold the League Covenant by whatever methods required (implying that might include military action).
- Source D mentions the secret negotiations that Britain (and France) had had with Italy; Source B does not.
- B suggests that Britain took the lead in opposing Mussolini by imposing sanctions; D does not suggest that Britain took the lead in this.
- B focuses on why Britain wanted to avoid war with Italy (prioritising other threats, weakness of the British navy); D does not refer to why Britain wanted to avoid war.

The IBO mark scheme is as follows for Question 3:

Marks	Level descriptor
5–6	The response includes clear and valid points of comparison *and* of contrast.
3–4	The response includes some valid points of comparison *and/or* of contrast, although these points may lack clarity.
1–2	The response consists of description of the content of the source(s), and/or general comments about the source(s), rather than valid points of comparison or of contrast.

4. Using the sources and your own knowledge, analyse the reasons for the League of Nations' failure to get Mussolini to end his invasion of Abyssinia. [9 marks]

2. CASE STUDY: GERMAN AND ITALIAN EXPANSION (1933–1940)

Source material that could be used:

Source A:
- Eden implies that not all members of the League favoured strong sanctions against Mussolini and that if sanctions had been enforced rigorously Mussolini might have been stopped. However, Eden arguably cannot be taken at face value as he is representing British policy as much firmer than it actually was.

Source B:
- Mussolini knew about British and French policy and their desire to avoid war because he had secretly intercepted their communications.
- Mussolini knew that Britain prioritised the Japanese and German threats over Italy.
- Britain had only just started to rearm.

Source C:
- Although the League did apply sanctions on Mussolini, they did not include oil.
- Mussolini did not take Britain and France seriously.

Source D:
- Britain had been reluctant to take action against Mussolini and was anxious to achieve a negotiated settlement.
- Britain and France secretly conducted negotiations with Italy to try to avoid war. Hoare suggests these were not sinister, but they did in fact did undermine the League.

Own knowledge that could be used:
- Britain and France secretly discussed giving Mussolini two-thirds of Abyssinia—the so-called 'Hoare-Laval Pact'. When news of this leaked out, the two ministers had to resign and Mussolini had confirmation that Britain and France would not use force to stop him.
- There was a 6-week delay before agreeing to impose sanctions.
- Non-members of the League continued to trade with Italy (Germany, the US).
- The League was slow to act—there was a requirement for unanimous decision-making.
- The League had not worked out the protocols for raising a peace-keeping force.
- Britain and France were keen not to push Italy too far, as they wanted to preserve the Stresa Front.
- The League was distracted in March 1936 by Hitler's remilitarisation of the Rhineland.

The IBO mark scheme is as follows for Question 4:

Marks	Use of sources	Own knowledge
7–9	Clear references are made to the sources, and these references are used effectively as evidence to support the analysis.	Accurate and relevant own knowledge is demonstrated. There is effective synthesis of own knowledge and source material.
4–6	References are made to the sources, and these references are used as evidence to support the analysis.	Where own knowledge is demonstrated, this lacks relevance or accuracy. There is little or no attempt to synthesise own knowledge and source material.
1–3	References to the sources are made, but at this level these references are likely to consist of descriptions of the content of the sources rather than the sources being used as evidence to support the analysis.	No own knowledge is demonstrated or, where it is demonstrated, it is inaccurate or irrelevant.

Apply the mark band that provides the **'best fit'** to the responses given by the candidate. While it is expected that there will be coverage of *at least two* of the sources, candidates are not required to refer to all four sources in their responses.

Appendix

References

Adamthwaite, Anthony P., 1979. *The Making of the Second World War*. London: Routledge.

Bartlett, C. J., 1994. *The Global Conflict*. Harlow: Longman.

Bell, P. M. H., 2007. *The Origins of the Second World War in Europe*. 3rd ed. Abingdon: Routledge.

Blinkhorn, Martin, 1984. *Mussolini and Fascist Italy*. London: Methuen.

Busch, Noel F., 1973. *A Concise History of Japan*. London: Cassell.

Costello, John, 1981. *The Pacific War*. London: Collins.

Crozier, Andrew, 1997. *The Causes of the Second World War*. Oxford: Wiley-Blackwell.

Delzell, Charles F. ed., 1971. *Mediterranean Fascism, 1919-1945: Selected Documents*. London: Springer.

Fry, Geoffrey K., 2001. *The Politics of Crisis: An Interpretation of British Politics, 1931-1945*. Basingstoke: Palgrave Macmillan.

Hane, Mikiso, 2001. *Modern Japan*. Colorado: Westview Press.

Henig, Ruth, 1985. *The Origins of the Second World War*. London: Methuen.

Henshall, Kenneth G., 2012. *A History of Japan*. 3rd ed. Basingstoke: Palgrave Macmillan.

Hitler, Adolf, 1925. *Mein Kampf*. Translated by Ralph Mannheim., 1969. London: London Hutchinson.

Kallis, Aristotle A., 2000. *Fascist Ideology: Territory and Expansionism in Italy and Germany, 1922-1945*. London: Routledge.

Keylor, William R., 1984. *The Twentieth-Century World and Beyond*. Oxford: Oxford University Press.

Kitchen, Martin, 2006. *Europe Between the Wars: A Political History*. 2nd ed. Abingdon: Routledge.

Knight, Patricia, 2003. *Mussolini and Fascism*. London: Routledge.

Knox, MacGregor, 1982. *Mussolini Unleashed, 1939-1941: Politics and Strategy in Fascist Italy's Last War*. Cambridge: Cambridge University Press.

Lamb, Margaret and Tarling, Nicholas, 2001. *From Versailles to Pearl Harbor: The Origins of the Second World War in Europe and Asia*. Basingstoke: Palgrave Macmillan.

Lee, Stephen J., 1987. *The European Dictatorships: 1918–1945.* London: Routledge.

Lee, Stephen J., 2003. *Hitler and Nazi Germany.* London: Routledge.

Mawdsley, Evan, 2009. *World War II: A New History.* Cambridge: Cambridge University Press.

Morgan, Philip, 1998. *Italy 1915–1940.* Bedford: Sempringham Publishing.

Overy, Richard, 1989. *The Road to War.* London: Stoddart Publishing.

Overy, Richard, 2014. *The Inter-War Crisis.* Revised 2nd ed. Abingdon: Routledge.

Parker, R. A. C., 1997. *The Second World War: A Short History.* Oxford: Oxford University Press.

Roberts, J. M., 1999. *Twentieth Century: A History of the World 1901 to the Present.* Allen Lane: London.

Ross, Graham, 1983. *The Great Powers and the Decline of the European States System: 1914–1945.* London: Longman.

Rothwell, Victor, 2001. *The Origins of the Second World War.* Manchester: Manchester University Press.

Royal Institute of International Affairs, 1944. Bulletin of International News, Vol. 21, No. 5. [online] Available at: <www.jstor.org/stable/25643578> [Accessed 21 December 2016].

Taylor, A. J. P., 1961. *The Origins of The Second World War.* London: Hamish Hamilton.

Tohmatsu, Haruo and Willmott, H. P., 2004. *A Gathering Darkness.* Oxford: SR Books.

Young, Louise, 1999. Japan at War: History-writing on the crisis of the 1930s. In: Gordon Martel, ed. *The Origins of the Second World War Reconsidered.* New York: Routledge.

List of figures

Figure 1.1	**Commodore Perry depicted in a Japanese woodblock.**	
	Source: Color woodcut by Roko, c. 1854, Chadbourne collection of Japanese prints, Prints and Photographs Division, Library of Congress (LC-USZC4-1307)	
Figure 1.2	**Emperor Meiji by Takahashi Yuichi.**	
	Source: Takahashi Yuichi (Artist), Imperial Collection [Public domain], via Wikimedia Commons/user:Maculosae tegmine lyncis	
Figure 1.3	**"China – the cake of kings and...of emperors".**	
	Source: Henri Meyer (Illustrator), Bibliotheque Nationale de France, via Wikimedia Commons/user:Pmx	
Figure 1.4	**Japanese print of the Battle of the Yellow River (1894) by Korechika.**	
	Source: Kobayashi Kiyochika (Illustrator) [Public domain], via Wikimedia Commons/user:PawełMM	
Figure 1.5	**Map of the battlefields of the Russo-Japanese War.**	
	Source: Russo-Japanese War: A Photographic and Descriptive Review of the Great Conflict in the Far East (P. F. Collier & Son, 1904) [Public domain], via Wikimedia Commons/user: Amagase	
Figure 1.6	**Foreign Minister Shidehara.**	
	Source: Orange3892 (Own work) [CC BY-SA 4.0], via Wikimedia Commons	
Figure 1.7	**The Lytton Commission inspecting the South Manchurian railway line.**	
	Source: Unknown photographer [Public domain], via Wikimedia Commons	

Figure 1.8	**Japanese rebels in February 26 mutiny.** *Source:* "Showa History Vol.7: February 26 Incident" (Mainichi Newspapers Company), Unknown photographer [Public domain], via Wikimedia Commons/user:Abasaa)
Figure 1.9	**The Emperor Hirohito at his coronation in 1928.** *Source:* Imperial Household Agency [Public domain], via Wikimedia Commons/user:Barakishidan
Figure 1.10	**Japanese troops entering Nanjing.** *Source:* Unknown photographer, German Federal Archives [CC BY-SA 2.0]
Figure 1.11	**Chiang Kai-shek.** *Source: Modern China: A Very Short Introduction* (Oxford University Press, 2008) [CC BY-SA 3.0], via Wikimedia Commons/user:WikiLaurent
Figure 1.12	**Japanese special naval landing forces in Shanghai.** *Source:* Unknown photographer, Ministry of the Navy (Brent Jones: Rising Sun in the East 1937) [Public domain], via Wikimedia Commons/user:Benlisquare
Figure 1.13	**Chiang Kai-shek (Jiang Jieshi).** *Source:* Unknown photographer, Library of Congress (LC-USZ62-39907), via Wikimedia Commons/user:Militaryace
Figure 1.14	**Chiang Kai-shek (Jiang Jieshi), his wife and General Stilwell in 1942.** *Source:* Captain Fred L. Eldridge (Photographer / Department of Defense), National Archives and Records Administration (ARC: 531135), [Public domain], via Wikimedia Commons/user:Ferengi
Figure 1.15	**Prince Konoe.** *Source:* <https://tanken.com/kokkai.html> [Accessed 11 October 2021>, Unknown photographer [Public domain], via Wikimedia Commons/user:Daffy123
Figure 1.16	**Japanese naval aircraft prepare to take off from an aircraft carrier to attack Pearl Harbor during the morning of 7 December 1941.** *Source:* Official U.S. Navy Photograph (80-G-71198), Unknown photographer [Public domain], via Wikimedia Commons/Alonso de Mendoza
Figure 1.17	**Roosevelt signing the declaration of war on Japan.** *Source:* Abbie Rowe (Photographer), U.S. National Archives and Records Administration (ARC: 520053) [Public domain], via Wikimedia Commons / user:Rambo's Revenge
Figure 1.18	**'Trial by Geneva'.** *Source:* David Low, *Evening Standard*, London (1932)
Figure 2.1	**King Zog of Albania.** *Source:* <http://www.bicephale-production.com/photo4105033.html> [Accessed 20 January 2017], Pietro Marubi (Photographer) [Public domain], via Wikimedia Commons/user:OLD ALBANIAN PHOTOS
Figure 2.2	**Benito Mussolini.** *Source:* <https://time.com> [Accessed 20 January 2017], Unknown photographer [Public domain], via Wikimedia Commons/user:К.Лаврентьев)
Figure 2.3	**Hitler (1933).** *Source:* Theo Eisenhart (Photographer), Bundesarchiv, Bild 183-S38324 [CC BY-SA 3.0 (http://creativecommons.org/licenses/by-sa/3.0/de/deed.en)], via Wikimedia Commons/user:DIREKTOR)
Figure 2.4	**Mussolini and Hitler, at the time of the Axis agreement, October 1936.** *Source:* Unknown photographer, Insituto Luce [Public domain], via Wikimedia Commons/user:MjolnirPants
Figure 2.5	**Neville Chamberlain (centre), on his visit to Hitler at Berchtesgaden in September 1938.** *Source:* Bundesarchiv, Bild 183-H12486 [CC BY-SA 3.0 de (http://creativecommons.org/licenses/by-sa/3.0/de/deed.en)], via Wikimedia Commons/user:Cropbot

Figure 2.6	**Edouard Daladier (French Prime Minister), leaving the Munich Conference, September 1938.**
	Source: Bundesarchiv, Bild 183-H13007, [CC BY-SA 3.0 de (http://creativecommons.org/licenses/by-sa/3.0/de/deed.en)], via Wikimedia Commons/Alonso de Mendoza)
Figure 2.7	**German bomber, part of the Condor Legion sent to Spain.**
	Source: Unknown photographer, Biblioteca Virtual de Defensa: Guerra Civil. Tomo II (MUE-202443) page 145 [CC BY-SA 3.0 (http://creativecommons.org/licenses/by-sa/3.0/de/deed.en)], via Wikimedia Commons/user:Aracali
Figure 2.8	**Hitler with Artur Seyss-Inquart, the Austrian Nazi leader.**
	Source: Unknown photographer, Bundesarchiv, Bild 119-5243 [CC BY-SA 3.0 de (http://creativecommons.org/licenses/by-sa/3.0/de/deed.en)], via Wikimedia Commons/user:Malus Catulus
Figure 2.9	**Chamberlain, Daladier, Hitler and Mussolini at Munich. Photo from Allgemeiner Deutscher Nachrichtendienst.**
	Source: Bundesarchiv, Bild 183-R69173 [CC-BY-SA 3.0 (http://creativecommons.org/licenses/by-sa/3.0/de/deed.en)], via Wikimedia Commons
Figure 2.10	**Stalin with Voroshilov.**
	Source: Unknown photographer [Public domain], via Wikimedia Commons/user:EugeneZelenko
Figure 2.11	**The launching of the German battleship, Tirpitz.**
	Source: Unknown photographer, Bundesarchiv, DVM 10 Bild-23-63-40 [CC BY-SA 3.0 de (http://creativecommons.org/licenses/by-sa/3.0/de/deed.en)], via Wikimedia Commons/user:Ras67
Figure 2.12	**Louis Barthou visiting Marshal Pilsudski in Warsaw, 1934.**
	Source: Genjusz niepodległości, Lwów 1935, page 33 [Public domain], via Wikimedia Commons/user:Andros64
Figure 2.13	**Maurice Gamelin, France's Commander-in-Chief, 1936.**
	Source: Photographie de presse de l'Agence Meurisse, Bibliothèque nationale de France [Public domain], via Wikimedia Commons (File uploaded by user: Kokin)
Figure 2.14	**Jozef Beck addressing the Polish Sejm (Parliament), rejecting Hitler's demands, May 1939.**
	Source: Polish state agency (PAT) newsreel, [Public domain], via Wikimedia Commons (File uploaded by user: Andros64)
Figure 2.15	**'The Prussian Tribute in Moscow'.**
	Source: "Mucha" weekly, [Public domain], via Wikimedia Commons (File uploaded by user: Julo)
Figure 2.16	**Polish infantry marching.**
	Source: Apoloniusz Zawilski (1972) "Bitwy Polskiego Września" Unknown photographer [Public domain], via Wikimedia Commons
Figure 2.17	**Map showing partition of Poland agreed by Germany and Poland; the map is signed by Stalin and Ribbentrop.**
	Source: Unknown photographer, via Wikimedia Commons
Figure 2.18	**German infantry attacking through a burning Norwegian village, April 1940.**
	Source: Bundesarchiv, Bild 183-H26353 / Borchert, Erich (Eric) / CC-BY-SA 3.0, via Wikimedia Commons
Figure 2.19	**Rotterdam centre after its destruction by German bombers on 14 May, 1940.**
	Source: US Defense Visual Information Center, Unknown photographer [Public domain], via Wikimedia Commons
Figure 2.20	**Aircraft spotter during the Battle of Britain.**
	Source: National Archives & Records Administration, Unknown photographer [Public domain], via Wikimedia Commons

Figure 2.21	**Heinkel He III bombers.**
	Source: Unknown author, Imperial War Museum [Public domain], via Wikimedia Commons
Figure 2.22	**President Roosevelt signing the Lend-lease Bill, May 1941.**
	Source: By Associated Press photograph. No. 21773. Forms part of: New York World-Telegram and the Sun Newspaper Photograph Collection (Library of Congress). [Public domain], via Wikimedia Commons
Figure 2.23	**Haile Selassie making a radio broadcast.**
	Source: United States Office of War Information, Library of Congress [Public domain] LC-USE6-D-008746
Figure 2.24	**Mussolini cheered by Fascist Youth in Rome, 1935.**
	Source: Unknown Photographer [Public domain], via Wikimedia Commons
Figure 2.25	**Mussolini & Hitler in Munich in September 1938.**
	Source: Bundesarchiv, Bild 146-1969-065-24 / CC-BY-SA 3.0
Figure 2.26	**Mussolini delivering his declaration of war speech, from the balcony of the Palazzo Venezia in Rome.**
	Source: Unknown photographer [Public domain], via Wikimedia Commons
Figure 2.27	**Ethiopian men gather, with captured Italian weapons, to hear the announcement of Emperor Haile Selassie's return in May 1941.**
	Source: Unknown photographer [Public domain], via Wikimedia Commons
Figure 2.28	**A cartoon in the Daily Dispatch, December 1935.**
	Source: The Daily Dispatch, December 1935